B7965
A Boy called Szmulek; a Man named Sam
Rik Arron

ISBN: 978-1-914933-63-9

Published By: -

i2i
PUBLISHING

i2i Publishing. Manchester.
www.i2i.publishing.co.uk

Sam, my promise to you was to share your story. In this book, my promise is now fulfilled. The privilege and honour were all mine, though. Your light shines so bright, despite those who attempted to extinguish it. Now your story can illuminate the whole world, forevermore. Thank you Sam for your courage, your vulnerability, your trust, your friendship, and your love.

Contents

5

Prologue

Wild Boys of World War Two

It's autumn 1945, just outside Munich. The sky is clear and the temperature is warm, although the sun remains hidden behind the distant mountains. Germany is still bristling from its recent defeat in the war, and everywhere feels eerily quiet and subdued.

Four smartly dressed young boys are walking side by side along the shore of a lake. They tease each other playfully and pass a cigarette back and forth along the line, taking a couple of drags each when their turn comes. The sound of their voices echoes around the deserted valley; they have the entire lake to themselves.

There are few places on planet Earth as beautiful as Lake Starnberger, a natural lake formed in a glacial hollow and set against the backdrop of the snow-covered Alps; the boys stop for a moment and take in the magnificence of the scene before them.

The tallest of the boys picks up a stone and hurls it up into the sky. The stone hangs in the air, reflecting in the glassy stillness of the lake surface; for a brief moment, there appears to be two identical stones, but in an instant these stones collide, and the surface of the water breaks out into a rippling cascade of circles. The other boys join in, throwing their stones higher and higher, competing with one another, daring to be bolder and higher than the throw before.

After a while, they tire of the game. The tallest, and oldest, steals the cap off the head of the smallest, and youngest, and runs off with it; the others give chase. They all run down the long wooden jetty that juts out into the lake, the sound of their boots thudding loudly against the ageing wood. When they reach the water's edge, they hurriedly take their clothes off, down to their swimming trunks, racing to be the first one ready to enter the water. The tallest boy wins and stands triumphant for a moment before taking a few strides back; he pauses, ushers the other boys aside with his hand and then takes a deep breath, launches into a sprint and then hurtles himself off the end of the jetty, turning a half somersault in the air before landing headfirst in the water. The other boys follow immediately, each of them pulling more and more daring dives and twists than the boy before them.

They swim, they paddle, they plunge, they dive. After a while, the three older and bigger boys get cold and drag themselves out of the lake to dry off and smoke another cigarette on the jetty. The youngest boy stays in the water by himself. He floats onto his back and looks up at the sky. He takes a slow, deep breath and basks in the majesty of his surroundings. He hears the sound of his friends talking on the jetty and the birdsong ricocheting out from the trees all around; he smells the smoke from the cigarette as it wafts out onto the lake and hangs in the air around him; but his thoughts drift elsewhere. Tears form in his eyes and trickle slowly down his cheeks into the salty lake water.

His name is Szmulek, although we will come to know him as Sam. He is just sixteen years old, but he looks much younger. He's not any ordinary sixteen-year-old boy, though. Just a few weeks earlier Szmulek was liberated from a concentration camp, one of many he had lived in for the previous two years, following four years in the ghetto in Lodz, Poland. Befriended by the other boys after liberation, all of them have been orphaned by the war and are far, far away from the homes they once knew. They are roaming around Europe trying to make sense of the new world they have been thrown into. Living in ghettos and concentration camps for the last five years has left them unsocialised, wild, feral. They are the wild boys of World War Two.

They aren't the only ones.

Introduction

Life-Changing Calls

I sat alone in my car outside the back of my office building, contemplating driving into the city for lunch. I wound the window down just enough to notice the faint scent of spring, finally in the air. I sat there for over an hour trying to get some space and clear my mind, my busy, anxious, claustrophobic mind.

I had escaped from the office because we were having to make redundancies in our thirty-five-year-old family business, and while the toughest decisions had already been forced upon us, I was finding it too difficult to sit amongst the very people whose lives I was going to have to turn upside down; people who I cared about deeply and who I presumed would also soon come to hate me.

I had scanned the radio stations searching for some salvation in a song but found cliches and triteness instead. So, I was sitting there in resolved silence when a call came in from an unknown number. I rarely, if ever, answer these kind of calls; it's usually somebody trying to sell me insurance or help me with an accident that I had never even been involved in, but without really thinking I just took the call, possibly hoping to change my ailing mood with any form of random distraction. Subsequently, I never made it into town.

"Hiya Rik, it's Robbie. How you doing mate?"

Robbie Gontarz and I knew each other through friends, having both grown up in the same suburb. Robbie was a year older than me in school though, and so our lives had always run somewhat parallel to each other and crossed only occasionally.

I hadn't spoken to Robbie on the phone before and even though my mind was tumbling into dark terrain, I felt an unexpected ease talking to him. Robbie has a warmth about him and a cheeky, Northern charm that is hard to resist. He asked if I minded him getting in touch. He had heard through our friends that I was a writer and he wondered if I had heard much about his dad's story. I had known that his dad was a Holocaust survivor with a harrowing past, but truthfully didn't know much more, and so, for the sake of my own personal distraction, I let Robbie continue.

For the next forty minutes, Robbie told me all about his dad's life in the concentration camps of Poland and Austria. Some moments he described in shocking, brutal detail while other parts he told me with broader brushstrokes. I sat in the car gripped by the unfolding story, each twist and turn seemingly taking a darker and darker path. By the end of the conversation, I was speechless. It was a story truly unlike any other I had ever heard. It had blown away the cobwebs of my own self-pity which I had been busy weaving. I was in total agreement with Robbie that he needed to get the story out there but wondered specifically why Robbie had called me.

And then he asked: Would I get involved and write the book?

To add impetus to his question he told me how his dad was almost eighty-eight and hadn't been very well recently. Time was running out. It was a cry for help rather than an attempt to lay any guilt on.

As a writer, and a lover of storytelling, every single cell in my body wanted to help tell this unbelievable story, but I was facing such intense challenges at that time in the family business, and my gut feeling was that I had to be honest with Robbie and tell him that as much as I wanted to do all I could to help him, I just wasn't in a position to handle the responsibility at that time. The story was too important, and I felt that I would let him and his dad down.

We chatted a little while longer and I gave him some advice on trying to find the right person to help him get the story told, but he was hesitant to trust somebody he didn't know with something so precious and dear to his heart.

We said goodbye and then I sat in the car for a few minutes to try and process the conversation. I watched the foggy blur of grey clouds skate across the city's flourishing skyline, and the hazy shape of the sun sitting patiently behind, waiting for its chance to burst on to the stage. I thought about Sam and all that he had gone through, and I considered how my own personal situation paled in comparison. I leaned into the rear-view mirror and stared into my own eyes, offered myself a motivating pep talk out loud and then walked back into the office to face up to things.

Following that phone-call, I spent the next few months helping to turn the business around. The redundancies had cut deep, not only with regards to the great team we had built over the years, but also into the otherwise impeccable legacy and heritage of the business. The business, selling leather jackets, had been started in the early 1980s by my mum and dad, more out of necessity than ambition, when my dad was made redundant from the business he had worked in since leaving school. They had built a true family business over the years, when my brother, and some years later I, joined the fold.

The upwards trajectory of the business carried on year after year, despite my dad's relentless fears of a downturn. His cruelly premature death in 2006 at just sixty years old, spared him the actual experience of his own gloomy prophecy, and so my mum, brother, and I were left to steer the business through the aftermath of the 2007 financial collapse and ensuing recession, without him.

We learnt on the job and rode the worst of it out, but fear can blunt the senses and we became numb to the dangers of the retail clothing sector, bludgeoning our way through with sheer bloody-mindedness. But, as our biggest customers pushed and pushed us, demanding more for less, we started to finally feel the pain. It was just a matter of time, one clumsy punch and we were floored.

We decided that a smaller, remodelled version of the business would allow us some space to breathe and reassess our priorities, and in my case, to address my key desire to spend more, and better, time with my family. It was the changes that we needed to make in order to achieve this new beginning at work and at home that I was contemplating when Robbie's call came in. It was now 2016.

After receiving Robbie's call, I never stopped thinking about Sam's story, though. It had stirred something inside me.

Robbie and I ran into each other once or twice after our telephone call, but the conversation never really veered beyond talking about work and football. Part of me was still scared to open up to the idea of getting involved with writing the story when I still wasn't yet in a position to dedicate the time and energy required to do it justice.

By the end of 2018 though, things were steadier in the business, my kids were now aged nine and five, and so life had become a bit less hectic. I was travelling back from work in the car one day and heard a discussion on the local radio station about an upcoming event to commemorate the Holocaust. My thoughts drifted immediately to Robbie and his dad, and so instinctively, I decided to call Robbie to see how he was and ask how he was getting on with his dad's story.

We had a long chat. As Manchester United fans, and with the team going through an atypically turbulent period, there was always something worthy of discussion. We put the footballing world to rights and then I asked how he was getting on with his dad's story. It was clear that they hadn't been able to move forward much in the years since we last discussed it.

Sam was approaching his ninetieth birthday and hadn't been in great health recently. I felt a sense of urgency in Robbie that he hadn't had before, but I was still nervous to commit fully to the project. I thought about it for a moment and then suggested to

Robbie that I could come over to meet his dad, bring some recording equipment with me, and at the very least, we could get Sam's story recorded once and for all on tape. I made it clear that I couldn't commit to anything more, I would simply get the story down and then Robbie could take it from there. In my mind, I considered that this would take an hour or so, maybe two at the very worst, and by doing that, I would have helped Robbie and Sam in some small way. It would be a good deed done to help out a friend.

At the very end of the conversation, Robbie mentioned that he was coming into town with his dad the following Wednesday for a Holocaust memorial at Manchester Cathedral and it would be a great chance to meet his dad. I hesitated, said I would put it in my diary, and politely said I'd do my best to be there. In all honesty though, I knew I had a busy week ahead and so didn't consider meeting at the cathedral a real possibility.

Those two seemingly random telephone conversations though would change our lives in ways that we could never know at that time. Almost a year to that very day, everything would change, forever.

***

The following Wednesday morning, I was busy at work, in and out of meetings, and with another one planned for just after lunch. I had ashamedly forgotten about meeting Robbie and Sam at the cathedral, when a reminder popped up on my computer screen to tell me that I should be meeting them in half an hour. I felt bad. I did want to meet Sam, having now heard parts of his tragic story, but I still had to prioritise my work in the business, and so I swatted the guilt away through the distraction of checking emails. One arrived that very moment. It was from the consultant due to meet me after lunch - he had to cancel at the last minute due to illness and could we rearrange?

I looked at my watch and realised that with the afternoon now clear, and with a quick march, I could make it into the city in time to meet Robbie and Sam. I grabbed my bag and coat and set off on what I determined to be the fastest route to the cathedral.

The same serendipity that made me call Robbie from the car was in play once again.

Manchester Cathedral is an incredibly beautiful building, inside and out. Nestled right in the heart of the city centre, it has remained a historical gem while all around it has become modernised and redeveloped. I walked into the vast central chapel of the cathedral, the midday sun was blasting through stained glass windows, painting the interior of the building with a kaleidoscope of dancing, rainbow hues. Casual visitors pottered about the atrium, gathering leaflets about local events, and reading the wall posters. In the very centre of the chapel, a small group of people stood around chatting. I spotted Robbie in the midst of the crowd, by his side was Sam. I waited for them to finish their conversation and then I waved to Robbie. Robbie was visibly surprised to see that I had made it and immediately ushered his dad over to meet me.

Sam, I would come to learn, never left the house without a baseball cap on his head; he was also notably small, and so swamped by the vastness of the cathedral, he appeared almost childlike. He shuffled over on his walking stick, and Robbie introduced us both. We decided to have lunch in the tea shop directly opposite the cathedral, where we could talk more privately.

We sat down at the table and pondered over the menu for a while. Sam removed his baseball cap to proudly reveal his impressive head of white hair, which he casually ruffled into some sort of style, and then he began to talk. Sam immediately called me Ricky, not a name that many people ever call me, I tend to get Rik or just the full version Richard. And, from the very moment he started talking, I was encapsulated by his warm and friendly manner. He had a sparkle in his eye, and a cheeky, mischievous smile. To put it simply, he was adorable. And I would soon come to discover that everybody that met him would feel exactly the same way about him.

We quickly discovered a connection through my late father and the golf club they had both been members of, and once I showed Sam a picture of my dad, he visibly relaxed. I was no longer just another stranger he was going to tell his story to, we were connected, and some important early trust was established.

I explained my plan to record his story using video camera equipment, and although we would film the story, it was just the audio we would be interested in. He nodded. I also explained to Sam and Robbie my existing commitments to the business and to my family; they both expressed understanding and gratitude for any involvement that I could possibly offer them. We finished up, offered hugs and goodbyes, and planned to meet again the following week for the first session.

Later that evening, Robbie called me. His dad was feeling really good for having met me, he felt relaxed in my company, and most importantly, he trusted me. He was ready to open up to me and tell me his story.

The following week, I cleared some time in my schedule and arranged with Robbie to go over to Sam's flat. I packed some basic camera equipment, intending to keep the setup as unintimidating as possible for Sam. Robbie met me outside the flat in the carpark and helped me in with my bags. He stopped me in the hallway just before we entered the flat and warned me of how difficult some of the things I was about to hear might be. I told him not to worry and that I was prepared; I had heard Holocaust stories before. Robbie raised his eyebrows and gave me one of his cheeky smiles.

Walking into Sam's flat was an experience in itself. It was small but perfect enough for Sam and his wife Sheila to live in. Robbie often stayed with them during the week, if he was working in Manchester and it was too far to commute from his family home in the Lake District. Sheila rarely made an appearance during the months of my visits, but her presence was always felt by the sound of the television coming loudly through the walls of her room. We moved down the short hallway corridor to the main room where Sam was waiting. The first thing I noticed as I stepped into the room was the incredible panoramic view that the flat had, overlooking Sam's beloved golf course.

"It's a nice view isn't it, Ricky? That's the reason I bought it in the first place," Sam said proudly.

Sam spoke perfect English but still with a very distinct Polish accent. His voice was raspy at times, a symptom not just of his age but also of the twice-weekly dialysis treatment that he had to undergo for the rest of his life.

The view was breath-taking, but it was the intense heat in the room that hit me the most. Robbie noticed, and with the cheeky grin and chuckle I would get to know only too well, told me his dad had the temperature like this all year round.

Immediately, I removed my coat and sweatshirt; it was always t-shirt weather in Sam's flat. I would forget this time and again in my future visits though, and constantly arrive over-dressed.

Sam was sat ensconced in a comfy, white, leather couch. He started to get up to greet me, but I headed straight over to greet him instead. We shook hands and chatted. He asked me about my family, and in particular how the kids were. He would do this every single time I saw him. He always wanted to know about my family, and not just the simple pleasantries of polite conversation; he wanted to know the details - the kids names, their ages, what they liked doing, how we spent time together as a family; he was genuinely interested. We talked easily while I set up the equipment, and within a few minutes, I was ready to record.

Chapter 1

Starched White Collars

I sat alongside the camera and talked directly to Sam, hoping he would soon forget the presence of the lens. I started the conversation with a gentle question about his first memories of his childhood. Sam shuffled awkwardly with his position on the sofa. He squeezed the cushions behind him and moved them into position behind his back. I sensed that he was feeling some trepidation about the conversation we were about to have, and so I told him to take his time. He smiled gently at me and then shuffled himself around a bit more. He finally settled into position and so I asked him again what his first memory was.

He smiled this time upon hearing the question, his eyes wandered to the sideboard directly opposite him across the room, and so I turned to see what he was looking at. Neatly laid out on the top of the sideboard was a resplendent tribute to his family in the form of faded, framed pictures. I would soon learn that these were his mother, father, sister and brother. With Sam slouched lowdown on the couch, his family appeared to loom over him. I sensed that this was both in a literal and spiritual sense, and most certainly intentional. Sam turned his gaze back to me. I prompted him once again.

I asked Sam to tell me about his first memories.

He began to talk:

My first memory was obviously seeing my parents, my family and my home. When I opened my eyes, that's what I saw. Well, that's what every kid sees when he's born. I think my first experience though must have been when I was about three, playing with the other kids.

Where we lived, it was a big complex of about sixty apartments, all Jewish, and in these apartments, the only non-Jew was the caretaker. I remember his daughter, who was about the same age as me, and we used to play together in the yard.

My first friends were all Jewish where I lived. I can still remember some of their names, although not all of them. It's seventy odd years ago … It's almost ninety years ago actually. Gosh. My, my (Sam chuckled).

I remember one friend. I can see him now. He was called Chil. He was a bit chubby. We always used to call him that nickname, in Yiddish, Chubby.

There was Moishe. I remember him. I can't remember what happened yesterday, but I remember Moishe. He was taller than us, and we were always playing hide-and-seek.

There was also a girl. She was our age, four and a half. She was called Renia.

It was a big complex. We are talking about sixty families, and the kids were all about the same age.

After that, I started going to Cheder to learn about the religion, and I acquired more friends from there, lots of friends as a matter fact. I don't remember them all, but visually, I do remember many of them. I just don't remember all the names. After several years of Cheder - I think I did three years - then, we started going to school.

In Poland, you started school when you were seven-years-old. The school was a mixed one. It wasn't just a Jewish school. It was for both Jews and non-Jews. I acquired lots of friends there, and we used to play out together. Some of them came to my home, and I used to go to theirs. Although it wasn't a ghetto, it was like one, because all the Jewish people lived together. So wherever I had to go to see my friends, it wasn't far. It wasn't like these days where the parents take the kids miles away to see their friends. We just walked. And that was the first few years of my life.

Sam seemed more relaxed already after this first brief visit into his childhood. He was smiling and there was a sparkle in his eyes; those memories were clearly happy ones.

I relaxed too. When he first began speaking, I had been concerned as to whether I had actually pressed record on the camera. I tried to hold Sam's gaze but kept darting to check the camera display. Once I knew I was good to go, I was able to maintain eye contact with Sam when he talked. I asked him about the actual place they lived in.

The place I lived in was in a big block, on the first floor. We only had one room. During the night, it was made into two beds because the settee turned into a bed. The kitchen was in one corner. It was all in one room. How we washed and cleaned ourselves was that my mother boiled some water in the kettle, and we used to have a Shizzle, and my mother would wash us from there. There were no facilities like we have now. Even then, there were some families that already had more conveniences, but we didn't; we were a relatively poor family.

We had a heater in the middle of the room. That was done by my father. He did it, and it was a pipe for a chimney going out through the window. So it was like a stove, and that gave us warmth. It wasn't that warm, but the best we could do.

I remember towards the end, my father separated the kitchen from the other part of the living room, by sort of doing it himself, so it wasn't a proper job. He did it so my mother could do the cooking in a separate place, rather than in the room where we all lived.

There was one bed which my father and mother slept in, and then we kids made our beds in the evening, or my parents made the beds for us from the couch. That's how we slept. As babies, I don't remember exactly what the situation was; we must have had some cradles or something. But as we grew up, they made a sort of bed for each of us, you know. But when my brother grew up, he was a bit older. He had a separate bed himself, in a corner so that he didn't sleep with us.

Then in the morning, when we all got up, my mother made sure everyone got washed and dressed. When we went to school, we had to be immaculate. If we weren't, the teachers would send us back home. I remember we had to have white starched collars on our shirt. Every week, my mother would wash it, and starch it, and iron it, and that's how we went to school. If I show you some photographs from school, I've got them somewhere, you would see how immaculate we looked, not in uniforms, which we didn't have, but in our own clothes and starched white collars. That was at every school in Poland.

Sam was in full flow by now. He was really relaxed, and although predominantly he maintained eye contact with me as he spoke, there were also moments where he looked up and away from me, lost in his nostalgia. I didn't always need to ask him questions; he skipped lightly from one subject matter to the next, then back again, as if the memories were just falling into him, and he couldn't get them out quick enough.

Chapter 2

A Happy, Happy Life

Sam sat forward and reached for a glass of water on the table in front of him, but it was tantalisingly just out of reach. The frustration showed on Sam's face. I felt myself reaching out to help him but then stopped myself and watched how he expertly rocked himself gently backwards and forwards and inched himself along the couch just enough so that he could reach the glass. He raised the glass and his arm shook, swirling the water around the lip. A few drops escaped and ran down his hand as he brought it closer to his mouth. He sipped lightly from the glass and swallowed slowly. Every movement he made was slow and mindful. He never seemed to be in a rush, possibly a habit forced on him by his ageing body, but to me, it seemed to come from a gentle and kind acceptance of himself. He put the glass down and worked his way back into a comfy position on the couch.

I asked Sam to tell me more about his family and the life they lived.

> My father was in the building trade. He didn't work on his own, he worked for somebody else. The money he earned was just enough. He had a family of five to keep, and it wasn't easy. So, the living conditions for us were relatively poor, but at the time, I wouldn't have noticed that. I was a happy child because the family gave me happiness.

We never argued, well maybe my sister and my brother might have had some differences sometimes, but overall, we never had serious problems. I remember my parents were always lovable to each other, and to us kids. Okay, there might have been occasions I was naughty, where I had to be put right, but I think that happens in general too.

The building itself, let me see. There were three separate blocks joined together on each side. Imagine going into a yard, and all the way around it are blocks of apartments. That's how it was. So, it gave us a chance to play in the yard, because it was overlooked by all the apartments. And I remember when we were playing, during the holiday times, whether a Jewish holiday or general holiday, just off school, we would play in the yard.

And, many times, from the first floor, to save me from going up to the apartment for lunch, my mother would make a parcel of a sandwich and throw it down from the first floor, for me to eat. It wasn't just me; all the kids were the same. They were given lunch thrown down from their various windows. I remember how we just sat down in a circle, all the kids, and we ate the sandwiches and had a picnic. Then, we carried on playing.

I asked Sam where the family bought all their food.

Shop-wise, at the front of each block was a corner shop which would serve that block or any other block. That's where my mother would go in the morning to get the milk and so on, sugar - whatever she needed. So, there weren't any big stores. Well, there were some big stores, but they were far away. I remember that there was enough good food to buy in the corner shop.

The street where I lived was called Kamienna, the number was 16. Each block of apartments had a big, big gate, because you didn't have cars in those days. So horses and carts were coming in with deliveries. Basically, that was our living conditions. They weren't elaborate, but for us kids, we were happy.

We lived on a cobbled street. There was no asphalt. At the end of it, you would come out from our block, and you turned left, and you would reach a main street called Kilinskiego. I still remember that; the name, and there were trams going on that street. I didn't use the trams because I walked to school. First of all, the tram was expensive, and secondly, it wasn't far to my school anyway.

If you turned right from the main street, you would face a big park, where they had slides and everything else that kids played with. I used to go there quite often, but we had problems sometimes being Jewish, because it was an open park for non-Jews as well. We were hassled by non-Jews, being called "bloody Jews," or in Polish, "Parszywy Zyd." It did bother us, but sometimes, if there was a lot of us, we did fight back. But if there weren't enough of us, we were cowards; we ran. Don't forget, Lodz had a population of about seven hundred thousand and there were two hundred and fifty thousand Jews, which is a third of the population. So really, although we weren't in a closed ghetto before the war, the area was like a ghetto because it was all Jews. In each block, we had a non-Jewish caretaker, who used to take care of everything we needed, keeping everything clean. And in general, overall, we had a very happy life.

I noticed Sam was using the phrase 'happy life' a lot in the opening minutes of our conversation. When he did so, it built a certain tension in me. I felt like he was unintentionally setting the stakes, and he was in some way preparing me, using the harsh contrast of this happy time with what, unknowingly for him at the time, was to follow. He seemed happy to talk about these memories though, smiling throughout, and although I didn't want to break his reverie, I wanted to know more about his family, and so tentatively, I asked him to talk about each of them.

My father was called Avrum, and he was, as I said, in the building trade. He left every morning and came back late at night. On Friday, he made sure he came back before the Shabbat, although we weren't that religious but compared to the Jewish life here now, we were. He would come home in time to get himself washed, cleaned up, and then, he would take us to synagogue.

My mother would be busy. Although we only had one room, that needed a lot of taking care of because there were five of us living, in and out, in and out. So, she always had something to do. She was called Ruchla. That's the Polish name again.

And I had a brother; he was four years older than me. He was called Srulek. That's the one you've seen on the picture there (Sam pointed to a frame on the mantelpiece in front of him).

He was grown up already from what I remember. In winter, he used to take me out on the sledges in the snow. I remember once, he nearly lost me. He was pulling the sledge, and I slid off, and he was still pulling it. Then I started shouting "Srulek, Srulek." He turned around and I was lying on the snow, and he came back. You know, there's certain things that stick in your mind and this I'll never forget. I mean, I must have been about, maybe six, seven at the time.

Then I had my sister, Sala. She was two years older than me. I remember at the school age, already, she was helping my mother to do a lot in the room, in our apartment or whatever it was.

So that's my family.

I asked Sam if he had any other family members outside of the five at home.

I had a relative in the same block: my mother's sister, and they were also a family of five. So we sometimes used to get together, especially on Shabbos and Yom Tovs. We got together, two or three families, and we celebrated Succot.

I also had an Auntie, another sister of my mother's, living on the next street on Killinskiego. We used to visit them and they would visit us. Although it was a small room like this, when they would come over, we all sat on the couch. And it was nice. It was a happy, happy life, you know. If you compare it to the life that we've got here, I mean it would be very primitive, but we didn't know anything else back then. All we really lived with, and wanted, was to be happy. And my family, and all the kids were all very happy. When I look at the pictures of my family, tears come to my eyes - what I've lost.

Sam looked down at his hands and sighed deeply. This was the first moment since we began talking where he paused to gather his thoughts. He breathed deeply, and then the conversation started up again from a completely different place. It was as if, over the years, he had learnt to develop an effective mechanism to cope, when the heavy emotions rose to the surface.

There were several kosher shops, because as I said before, it was a Jewish area with lots of short streets. Each area had two or three kosher shops. There was a kosher butcher, and a kosher fishmonger.

As a kid, I used to walk on Shabbat after dinner. First thing in the morning, we went to synagogue. Then we came home, and I used to go to the bakery which was facing us on the same street, to pick up the chulent, because we took it there on Friday before Shabbos. I remember the Chulent, which was like a stew, and my mother would have a newspaper on top of it. It would be in a big pot tied with string around it. We used to take it to the bakery, leave it there, and pick it up hot the next day. And the bakery put a stamped piece of paper with the name on it, you know, so you could pick it up and remember whose was whose. I used to carry the shizzle home, and then we had Shabbos dinner.

After that, I used to go out with some of my friends from the same block. We used to go to the main street. The road was called Piotrkowska, which is a beautiful, beautiful street. It's still in existence; I've seen it on the internet. They already had modern shops, but we never used to buy there because it was expensive. But, I remember going there, and we looked into them through the revolving doors, which we couldn't see in our part of the community. We would look in and imagine what it would be like to be rich and to go in shops like that.

There were pictures there, or cinemas as we call them these days, which now and again, I went to with some of my friends. We didn't go on Shabbos, but sometimes in the summer, after school, in the long days, because you used to be allowed out until about ten o'clock. I can't remember going to the pictures with my parents though. What I do remember were some Jewish theatres my parents took me to, though very seldom, you know, a few times, but I didn't particularly enjoy it. I preferred to go to the cinema, because some of the Jewish theatres, were very solemn and tragic, everything was sadness, and there was no happiness. But they shlepped me there; they shlepped the whole family when we used to go.

I smiled at Sam's use of Yiddish; the Yiddish words always seem so perfectly descriptive, even if you don't know exactly what they meant. Shlep has become quite a commonplace word these days, but hearing it coming from Sam's mouth, a ninety-year-old Jewish, Polish grandfather, it sounded so much more authentic. As if reading my mind, Sam typifies the image further with a gentle shrug of his shoulders followed by the phrase:

Thank God! It was not that often.

***

I was often amazed at the incredible detail with which Sam could remember things; names and places. The memories he was describing were almost eighty years old, yet they were still vivid and fresh in his mind. There was happiness in his voice and a smile on his lips when he spoke; I sensed that he could have stayed in these memories forever.

I had relaxed a lot more too; although there was always the thought in the back of my mind of what was to come, I was captivated now by Sam's happy energy, and I wanted to know more and more about this time of his life. So, I asked him what kind of things he did with his friends.

Occasionally, there were fairs in the park. I can't say how often it was, but it was monthly or quarterly, and we used to go quite a bit. They were marching the Polish soldiers, and playing music on certain occasions, which was either a Christian holiday or a general holiday. We used to stand, and watch, and listen to them.

We didn't have swimming pools when I was a kid. In the summer, there were ponds, not a pool or a lake or anything, just ponds, and we went swimming there. And I remember that we used to get these things from the water. What do you call them? Leeches, and they latched onto us and we had to keep picking them off. That's where I actually learned to swim, because I didn't see a pool until I came to England. We did that quite often with the boys.

I never went out on my own, always with the gang. You know, like here, we always had a clique. You've got lots of friends but also lots of acquaintances, and that's exactly what we had there. I had lots of acquaintances from Cheder, and from school, and from the yard, but just a few close friends and we were together all the time. They were in my apartment and I went to theirs.

There was a communal hall on the top floor, above us. It wasn't a big one, but we used to get together there with the other kids. If the weather was bad, we would go up there and play, and there were certain things, I don't know who donated them, but there were certain toys that we used to play with. The room was about four times the size of this, and that came in useful, because winter there lasted from September to the end of March. Sometimes, the snow never left. I believe it's different now, but in my time, it was very cold going to school. We would be in snow up to here, jumping from the first floor. We raced to see who would jump furthest. As kids, we did it, but now I'd get killed. Yeah, we played the daring games.

I remember there was a communal basement, and it was dark, and we dared each other to go down there, and we just shouted out our names to each other to know that we were there. That was a game to us. It was very primitive.

There was a warehouse in the yard too, a company that produced washing powder, I think. So there was a ramp where the horse and carts kept coming into the yard to deliver stuff to them. Sometimes, they wanted us kids to help with certain things. So they gave us five groschen, and five groschen would be, you know, so we could maybe buy an ice cream with it. I remember in the summer, we used to do some jobs for them, carry little parcels and so on, and it was cheap labour, but for us, it was extra money because our parents gave us very little. I think they gave us ten groschen in a week, so yeah, it was something additional to do in the yard.

My brother, who was four years older than me, joined a Zionist party, and that was on Pietkovska. It was called Baitar. He took me once. I've got a picture of it, although not here. I can find it somewhere and I can show it to you. He was the leader of the youth at Baitar; it was very impressive.

He was a very strong Zionist, although he was very young. But I remember that he had friends coming to the house, and they discussed politics, or Israel. It wasn't Israel at the time, it was Palestine. So, I didn't take part in it because I was too young. I remember there were actually strong arguments. You see, certain things keep coming back to me. He discussed things with my father, and they didn't argue, but my father was a left bund, which is here probably Labour, and Srulek was more Baitar, you know. But they always discussed it very strongly. I kept out of it. It didn't make any difference because all I wanted to do was play.

Sam began to cough and struggled to clear his chest. This happened quite a lot during the sessions; a side effect of his dialysis treatment. He felt the need to apologise every single time though. Sometimes, the coughing would make him forget his train of thought, and I could see him reaching to remember where he was up to. I asked him whether he had any idea what was going on in the outside world at that time.

None at all. Then when the war came and I was ten years old, I was in the third year of school. So really, all my knowledge that I acquired about what was going on, which was limited anyway, was after the war, not before or during the war. During the war, the kids never got any news. We got rumours, but they weren't correct rumours of the world; they weren't backed by anything.

Before the war, we heard our parents discussing it. Our relatives would come to visit us, or we would go to visit them. And they would discuss the war, but we kids didn't take any notice, because a kid doesn't absorb it, and does not think it will happen. So, we didn't take much interest in what they were talking about. What we heard was if the Germans invaded Poland, that the Jews would be the first to go.

Chapter 3

Thank God it's Not Me

Intentionally, I didn't do any research before I visited Sam for my first conversation. I wanted to be a blank slate, so that I could hear his story clearly, without my own knowledge getting in the way. I had a general understanding of the key events of the war and the events of the Holocaust, essentially from a couple of documentaries and films I had seen over the years and the information I was told as a kid.

Growing up, the man who lived in the house opposite me was a Holocaust survivor, Meyer, and although he never talked about it in any detail directly to me, I was made very aware of what his situation was from being very young. He was a gentle, sweet man who always said hello whenever he saw me, but he never spoke about his experience in the Holocaust. And then, one day I was sitting in the school hall at assembly with all the other kids from the school, and the headmaster said we had a very special guest who was going to tell us his life story. Then, Meyer walked in. I can remember elbowing my friend and excitedly telling him, "That man lives opposite me!" For the next half hour, he told his horrifying story of being a child in the concentration camps. The entire hall was hauntingly silent afterwards as Meyer took a bow and was escorted from the room by the headmaster.

A few weeks later, when I saw him in the street and we got talking, he rolled up his sleeve and showed me the numbers tattooed on the back of his forearm; it had faded heavily through the years as Meyer had grown, but it was still evident. I thought of him as something of a hero after that.

And so, essentially through Meyer's story, I was always distinctly aware of the Holocaust and understood that it was a truly dark period in human history, and one that must never be repeated. However, I'm from the 'charity relief' generation, whereby some of the worst horrors in the world can seemingly be solved by wheeling out a few celebrities, hosting an event and throwing money and donations at most problems.

I'm not necessarily proud of that rather selfish approach, but my generation hadn't really encountered any great tragedies, other than what we saw on our TV sets, and I think it gave us a certain lack of empathy. Everything bad that happened generally still only happened to other people.

The closest thing citizens of my home city, Manchester, had ever known about anything like this was in June 1996 when the IRA had bombed Manchester city centre. Thankfully, nobody was killed in the incident, and it sparked a long overdue makeover for the city, so even that wasn't thought of as being too bad.

But, sitting there with Sam was the first time in my life when I had felt the power of hearing someone else's tragic story unfold, and just listening was a humbling experience.

I asked Sam what happened next.

I remember Friday the 1st of September. I was at school in a class of about twenty kids. They had quite comfortable classes in Polish schools, actually. By about eleven o'clock, we heard the sirens going. We heard them before that, when we were at home, but they were just a try-out, you know. Anyway, this time, we heard them again, followed by bombardment from the aeroplanes. Then we realised that it was something serious. We still didn't realise about the actual war and what was going to happen to Jews, but we knew that this was now for certain. This was not a practice. So, we started getting worried. The teachers told us to hurry up and go home, and on our way, we heard the bombs. Every time a bomb fell, we thought it was very near us.

When I got home, in the yard, there were groups of people talking. I met my mother, my brother, and my sister; my father wasn't home yet. I remember my mother telling us, ordering us in fact, to get up to the apartment, close the door, shut the windows, and stay there until they came up. My mother stayed there talking to the neighbours.

Later, she came up and told us what had happened, that Germany had invaded Poland, not Lodz yet; and we may have a problem, because of being Jewish. They already had heard of the Kristallnacht in Germany, but we didn't know about it, or we didn't take any notice yet. When she came up to the apartment, she wasn't crying, but she looked shaken. She just tried to settle us kids. "Don't worry too much, but the war has started, and we hope that everything will be okay," she told us. There was no further discussion. We could see that there were tears in her eyes.

After that, we stayed in the room the whole day and the bombardment continued. Every time a bomb dropped, it sounded like it was next door. Although, thank God it wasn't, but it sounded like it.

Towards late afternoon, my father came home. Of course, he already knew what was happening. I remember my mother and father getting together, and they started to talk. I wasn't listening in to their conversation, but they sounded very, very worried.

In the days that followed, there was no school, and I remember I went out because food became very scarce, straight away, even before Lodz was invaded.

One day, I went to get a loaf of bread, because most of the shops had closed and we didn't have any stuff. As soon as the war started, there was no stuff delivered anywhere. But I went on to Killinskiego. There was a big shop, and I queued for bread. As I got near the door, which meant I would be served within the next minute or two, all of a sudden, somebody grabbed the back of my collar and pulled me out. "You Jews have to wait until we are served," he shouted at me. And that wasn't a German, that was a Pole. So, I got to the end of the queue again, which must have taken another half hour to three-quarters of an hour, and they had sold out. That repeated itself several times. So, each one of us in the family went to a different shop to see if one of us could get bread. That was the main thing, to get this bread. My brother, I think, managed to get some after two or three days. My sister tried; she couldn't. I tried again; I couldn't. That carried on for several days.

My father stopped working, and my mother didn't work anyway; she was a housewife. Most of the women didn't work. They kept the house, whether it was a big house or small house, and they stayed at home because they had the kids to look after. It wasn't like these days.

Anyway, several days later, the worst happened, Lodz was invaded by the Germans. And they immediately incorporated Lodz into the Third Reich. All the laws, including the laws for the Jews, became like in Germany, and they started harassing and murdering Jewish people.

It started off with them invading apartments. They dragged people out, men mainly, or young boys, teenage boys, put them into open carts, and took them away, and all those who were taken away, never came back. We didn't know but there were lots of rumours all the time as to where they were going to, another place, to a camp, but the camp wasn't described. There was no description of gas chambers, crematoriums, or anything like that, just the rumour about a camp.

So, we lived with that, and thank God my family wasn't taken away. My father and my brother were still there, although, my brother tried to escape, but later on. After several days, most of the men tried to leave Lodz and go towards Warsaw. Warsaw hadn't been taken at the time yet, but halfway walking towards Warsaw, they were met by the German army. Warsaw was now taken, and all the men came back.

There were joint owners of the apartment block where I lived. One was Jewish and the other one was a Volks Deutcher, which is a German living in Poland. One day, three or four Gestapo men came into the yard on motorbikes, dressed in Gestapo uniforms, including him. I was actually in the yard. I looked at him but I couldn't make out who it was. One of them shouted, "All Juden Raus," which meant all Jews out. But there wasn't anybody else there; it was all Jews. When I looked at him, I realised that this was the man who came every Friday to collect the rent for our apartment. And when I was a little boy, he used to pick me up, cuddle me, and even sometimes, give me a kiss. I couldn't believe that this was the man, the Gestapo man, who kicked us all out from the apartment. He gave all the Jews about two hours to leave.

We went to live on Kilinskiego, to a relative of mine, another sister of my mother, Zipporah. Don't forget in Poland, they had big families, lots of sisters and lots of brothers. They were a family of five as well. They also lived in one room, but it was bigger than the one we lived in. Now, we were ten people, but between the two women, they tried to keep us as clean as possible, as neat as possible, and to look after us as much as possible. It wasn't easy, but they managed to do it.

When one of us went out to do a bit of shopping, and we came back with some food, it was immediately distributed amongst the whole family of ten. It was never much, but what we had was evenly distributed. We were always close, as families.

We didn't play as much as before the war, for the simple reason that once the Germans invaded Lodz, it became incorporated into the Third Reich. From then on, at the time I was living with my aunt, the Germans would raid our yard. They came in, ordinary soldiers, German soldiers, about ten of them, pick out some Jewish young men, ask them to line up, and they would tie their hands behind their back with rope that they had brought with them. Then, they punched them until they were bleeding. Then, they knifed them with bayonets, and when they fell down, they shot them. Finally, they walked out laughing. If we were still in the yard playing, we were absolutely shocked and frightened. We hung on to one another.

After that, we went up to the room, where my mother had already seen it all from the window. No one dared to go on down to try and help or anything.

Another occasion was when a few wagons came into this same yard, jeeps actually, two or three with machine guns, and they raided the Shtiebel. Do you know what a Shtiebel is? If they don't have a proper synagogue, this is where Jewish people make a private one, a Shtiebel. They've got a Torah, and everything else. So, they raided that; it was on the ground floor. There were about twenty men on that morning service, morning prayer. They raided it and shot them all, set fire to the old religious things, books, bibles and then left, again, laughing. Every time I saw an atrocity against Jewish people, It never seemed as if the soldiers were on a job or doing it because they had to. It always looked like they enjoyed it.

We were shocked and frightened and shivering; but it didn't take long, because after seeing more of these sorts of things, we got conditioned to it, and we became like zombies. After several weeks, or maybe several months, it didn't bother us. I had a saying in my mind during the whole six years, 'Thank God it's not me, thank God it's not me'. I don't know whether that helped me or not, but that's what I kept saying.

These atrocities lasted all the time until we got into the ghetto. But during that time, when we were still living outside the ghetto, they made the Jews wear yellow stars, as you know, and those who didn't either wear a yellow star or those that tried to hide were immediately shot.

The Germans seem to have had authority, each soldier could do what he wanted to the Jews. He didn't have to answer to anybody. He did exactly what he wanted. They learned it either in the Hitler Youth, or in the Nazi movement.

And then, they had the caretakers collecting the bodies. This was all before we went into the ghetto. So, this period lasted from the middle of September until the end of 1939, and then they formed the ghetto.

We had very little food; it became scarce. They started rationing, but it had no value, because you went with your cash to the shops but there was no food.

The living conditions deteriorated. So a lot of us weren't as clean as we were before the war. There was no going to school with starched collars anymore for instance. It was a very primitive life altogether.

The days were very uncomfortable, but also once the Germans had incorporated Lodz into the Third Reich, they started burning all the synagogues. There must have been over two hundred and fifty synagogues in Lodz. I've got pictures on the internet from before; they were beautiful buildings and they were all burnt. All Jewish schools were closed.

The Jews were immediately forbidden to do anything or go anywhere. No schools. No synagogues, no clubs or anything. All these places were closed immediately. Even the yard wasn't safe, because as I said, the raids came in very often. I have only given you one or two instances about when they came in and picked out the young boys, and stabbed them, and shot them, and then about raiding the Shtiebel, but there were raids like this every day for different things. They had their lorry outside in the street. They never drove it in because it was too big to go through the gates, so they shlepped the people out. They came in with their guns and caught the men and took them away in the lorries.

Actually, my brother escaped once because there were rumours, you know, that young people should try and get to Russia. So, he tried to escape with some of his friends from Baitar, the organisation that he belonged to. Unfortunately, they were caught and put in a camp in Poland. I don't know what camp it was, because he came back after several days. He managed to escape and I remember, every time there was a raid, my parents had to hide him, because the Germans must have had a picture of him. So, thank God, he stayed with us until we went into the ghetto. From what I remember, he was sent into this camp, but it mustn't have been a camp like Auschwitz or Birkenau or anything, because the fact was that he and his friends managed to escape, so it couldn't have been that bad. I don't know how they escaped. He probably told my parents. I don't know.

The atrocities happened every day. They were hanging people, Jewish people. It was only Jewish people they did it to. The hangings took place on Plac Wolnoszczi. I remember the name. it's like a square in Lodz. They had the gallows for about twelve people, picked up in different apartments, and they were accused of being spies or something. They made us watch the hanging. That's when, as I said, I got conditioned to that way of life. It didn't matter to me. After that, when I saw dead bodies, it didn't matter. If I see a dead body now I go mad. I can't see a dead body now, but then it didn't matter. Right through the camps until the liberation, I was like that, and all that I kept thinking was, 'Thank God it's not me; thank God it's not me'.

Half an hour had passed where Sam had just talked without interruption, telling Robbie and I about this traumatic time when the Germans invaded Poland and in particular, Lodz. At times, Robbie looked at me with raised eyebrows, and I would offer a shrug and an awkward smile. It wasn't meant to be a smile, I was trying to show empathy but there comes a point with stories like this where you no longer have the emotional vocabulary of gestures and expressions to do justice to what you are hearing. I hadn't heard anything yet.

Chapter 4

Songs and Cigarettes

It dawned on me an hour into talking to Sam that I had totally misjudged the depth of his story. Naively, I had thought that we might get the entire story down in an hour or so. This assumption probably came from when Robbie mentioned to me over the phone that his dad had done a talk at the university recently and the talk had lasted an hour, including some questions from the audience. I wasn't in any particular hurry that day, but I had a lot going on with family and work, and so my mind was split, half on listening intently to Sam and the other half on everything else I had to do that day.

I've practised meditation for over thirty years though, and so I've come to know quite well how my mind works. I sensed that the distractions my mind was offering up were a kind of defence mechanism against the horrors of what I was hearing. It was a coping device. What Sam was describing was alarming and so my mind tried to deflect this incoming fear by offering up a to-do-list of meaningless tasks. I caught myself in the midst of this process several times that morning, and so, with the knowledge of my experience, I offered these distractions some gentle acceptance, allowing them to exist without getting caught in them. I took a deep breath.

I asked Sam, what happened next.

Well, then the ghetto started, I suppose. I can't remember the exact date really, because it was over a period of time. It was the end of 1939 or beginning of 1940. They ordered us out from the apartments, and we had to walk to the ghetto. We walked through the gates. It was the most dilapidated part of town. The ghetto wasn't surrounded by barb-wire yet, that came later, but we walked in; we met up with the Jewish police. They were already organised, because there was one man who was put in charge of the ghetto, that was Chaim Rumkowski; they called him the Elder of the Jews,. He was ordered by the Germans to coordinate everything in the ghetto. He organised the police, the Jewish police, and they coordinated everything for everybody that came into the ghetto. They asked us questions, our names and everything. You had to register like you're going into a hotel. So, we registered.

They allocated you a room, not an apartment, a room. So, we had a room for five. I would compare it to the size of this room here. I remember there was a couch, a cooker and a couple of stools, and that's it, and a bed. It looked like the bed was going to collapse any minute, you know, and that was for the five of us. So thank God we went in just as a family of five. We weren't together with our relatives anymore because they were allocated separately.

As we walked into the room, we tried to make ourselves comfortable and sat down. We didn't know what to do and what to say, so we just gazed at the walls. Then we had to find out what was happening. I remember it well. My father went down, he spoke to a Jewish policeman and asked, "What's next?" They said, "Well, when you came in we asked you certain questions because we have to know. We will try to allocate certain jobs for each one. So, we'll come to your address when we are ready, and allocate you a job. That's where you'll be working as long as you're in the ghetto." So, my father came back. He told us what they had said, and we waited, and we waited. I don't think we waited long, a few days maybe. Then, two policemen came and allocated us jobs.

My brother and I were allocated a place called Satler resort. I made harnesses for the German horses, and we were doing it all by hand. There were two needles, and you had to make a hole and get it through. It was hard work, believe me, as a kid especially. If the stitches were wrong when they came to examine them, they hit you over your head with a rubber truncheon.

Srulek was in a different room, so I don't know exactly what he did, but I think he did the same thing as me. My mother was allocated something in the kitchen. My sister was allocated to the hospital. They created a hospital, not that it was any good, because nobody came out. My father, being a builder, was allocated building work, but outside the ghetto, so he was picked up by a jeep in the morning, taken out to do his work and brought back at night. And when we asked him what it was like, he always said it wasn't too bad, because he got food, and the work was the same as he did before the war, so really it wasn't that bad for him.

I remember, thinking back, to sitting on a stool selling cigarettes in the summertime when it was light in the evenings, when I came home from work. I remember my brother made me a trestle and a chair to sit down outside our building, on the street actually outside in the yard. Somehow, I managed to get contacts to buy cigarettes, smuggled cigarettes which I sold. This helped the family, because the extra money could buy smuggled food, and whatever else you couldn't buy. It had to be smuggled as everything was rationed. I got the contact, because as a kid, you are inquisitive, you know. You try, you asked questions, and so on. I met some grown-ups, and they sort of helped me. They said that if I wanted the stuff, I'd have to pay in advance, so that's what we did.

The money was ghetto money, ghetto marks. It was a black market of dollars, like it always is everywhere. So, my parents had a few dollars still when they came into the ghetto. I told them about the cigarettes and they gave me some money. I can't remember how much it was, and I paid these people in dollars, and they supplied me with the cigarettes. So, I was sat outside every evening in the summer, and I sang some songs, and people came along and bought the cigarettes from me. I made some money. It didn't make me rich, but what I made helped the family. We did manage to buy some extra food.

When I think about it now, I think I always had that business mind. I was an entrepreneur even when I didn't know that I was. I will tell you the stories later of how this business mind would help me in so many ways.

Chapter 5

Chutzpah comes in Handy

One sunny spring afternoon, just as we were finishing off our filming for the day, Sam told me the story about how he had established himself in business.

He leaned in towards me, as if he was revealing secrets.

Sam, in Manchester for just over a year, was living with three of his friends in a small flat above a shop on Leicester Road, a heavily Jewish area of North Manchester. They all needed to get out and find their own space; they got on really well as friends but there were occasions when the limited space caused some friction amongst them, and they thought independence was the best way forward, for all of their sakes.

Sam had managed to find a job working in a bedding factory in Cheetham Hill, folding pillows and sheets all day long. It was steady, honest work that gave him an income but he needed something else and so he started asking around.

He got a job working for a German Jew making leather shaving kits. He worked hard and felt he did a good job and so one day, he thought it was time to ask his boss for a raise. The German looked him up and down and said he didn't deserve a raise yet, and so Sam just walked out; he said it felt great to have the freedom to walk away from a German without any further repercussions.

It was a small victory, but he found himself unemployed again.

Resourceful and cheeky as he was, Sam convinced a guy he met through a friend to give him a job in his factory down Cheetham Hill Road. Ironically, it was making handbags and working with leather once again, a poignant coincidence that wasn't lost on Sam.

Sam watched the other workers as they crafted the bags, by hand. He studied their pattern making, he marvelled at the way they cut the leather with their huge scissors and knives, he watched the way they used the glue to piece the sections together, and he noticed the intricacies of their hand stitching.

His own ability grew steadily, and with his growing confidence, he hatched a plan in his mind to branch out on his own and start his own factory.

With everything Sam had been through, he understood that opportunities were something that you made happen and didn't wait around for.

The first thing he did was ask about an empty attic he had heard about above his favourite bakery, Jacob's Bakers. After a short bit of negotiating, Sam convinced the landlord to let him have the room for free - such was Sam's irrepressible charisma.

He managed to do the same thing with the sewing machine manufacturer, Singer, and the wholesaler who sold him the leather; they both agreed to let Sam pay them back in instalments once he had started to generate income.

Now he had everything he needed to start his own factory, the only problem was he had never made a bag from scratch before, previously using the patterns and pieces already prepared for him. He had also never used a sewing machine before.

Nevertheless, uninhibited, Sam began.

He cut the shape of what he thought a handbag looked like and, using the knowledge he had acquired, he put together his very first bag. It took him the entire week, but he felt proud of it; he thought it looked good.

From nowhere, a man named Leslie Star, appeared in his attic. Leslie owned a factory of his own and he had somehow heard about Sam's exploits. He loved the bag Sam had made and wanted to buy it, and anything else that Sam could make. It was a lucky break; although Sam would often say that luck was something that we create for ourselves through our endeavour.

Leslie and Sam built up a great relationship. The word got around about the quality of Sam's bags and this brought him to the attention of a man called Frank Howley, a successful businessman who owned a large factory in Ancoats, a district on the outskirts of Manchester city centre steeped in history and industry. Frank was a straight-talking guy. He didn't mince his words and offered Sam a partnership there and then.

Sam couldn't refuse.

Over the next few years, Frank and Sam built up a great business together. Sam oversaw the manufacturing, and even still made some of the bags himself, but, more importantly, he learnt the ins and outs of running a big business. He learnt to use his character and charisma to build great relationships with customers and suppliers; he had, in bucketloads, what was called 'Chutzpah'. With his honesty and integrity, he learnt how to be firm but fair in business. And, with great compassion and empathy, learnt from his life experiences so far, he created deep and lasting loyalty with his workers.

But those life experiences had also created an insatiable drive in Sam, a purpose, a mission to do something great with his life - he wanted a family of his own and to provide for them in ways that he could never have even dreamed of as a child. And so, Sam decided to venture out on his own and create a business and a legacy that would help him fulfil his ambitions, and, with Frank's blessing, he set about fulfilling his dream of finally becoming a successful, independent businessman.

And he did.

And, as destiny seemed to relentlessly persist, it would inevitably be manufacturing leather goods.

The serendipity of Sam's business path is further echoed to this very day as Robbie also owns his own business, based in the Lake District, unsurprisingly, manufacturing leather goods.

Chapter 6

The Bloody Police

Sam reached for his glass of water. He had placed it on the very edge of the table and so with just a few shuffles, he was able to retrieve the glass and take a sip of water. He held on to the glass this time, resting it on his leg, and expertly resumed his story from the exact place he had left off.

> Anyway, when we all came home at night, we were always knackered. So, we sat down wherever we found a seat to sit, and either fell asleep, or if we felt like it, we would discuss things. But we didn't discuss the atrocities, because each one of us thought talking about it would make it worse. In fact, from what I remember, it didn't make it worse because I lost normal human thinking completely. It didn't matter to me, because as I mentioned, on the cobblestones walking in the streets, we had seen dead bodies, and I just passed them by. It wasn't just me. I could see other people just passing them. They might just have a look, and walk home, because they didn't collect the bodies during the day; they only arranged to collect the dead bodies during the afternoon, or evening, or night. They collected them with the horse and carts and took them out. They were buried in a communal cemetery just outside the ghetto. Half the Jewish cemetery was in the ghetto, and a half was outside.

I don't know exactly how big the ghetto was. It was pretty big. Don't forget that initially, there were a hundred and fifty thousand people all crammed into the living accommodation, but it still took a hundred and fifty thousand. And you had to have different factories and so on, because there were the factories like the one my brother and I worked in, making the harnesses. But there were other factories making German uniforms and others making ammunition. There were lots of factories, you know, so it had to be reasonably big, but not just for the living accommodation.

Initially, we thought that Rumkowski would help us and this is controversial because a lot of people still think he was fantastic. In the ghetto, the only time we saw the soldiers come in is when they raided us, but ordinarily, we only saw Jewish police. At first, they might have been sympathetic to us. Like I said to you, when they provided us with jobs, they were still human beings, but after several months, they weren't. I think it's in the nature of a human that he can change in certain conditions. I didn't think of that at the time of it but thinking about it now, I know because it didn't happen to just one person or two, it happened to all of them. They all seemed to change. They were more bombastic to you; they were hostile. If you don't do it, we'll dispose of you, or something, you know. I think when they took this job, they were also taught by the Germans how to handle us, and if they didn't handle us the way the Germans wanted, then they feared for their life as well. At first, as I said, they were helping us, but when they started getting hostile, we would complain. "The bloody police, the bloody police, they are like the Germans," we'd say. It was like it in the camps too, which we'll come to later. We're not in the camp yet, but the Kapos in the camp were the same. They started out probably very decent but couldn't keep it up. They wanted to survive.

At this point, several hours into our first conversation, Sam began to look tired. I looked at Robbie; he had sensed it too. "Shall we call it a day, dad?" Robbie asked. Sam nodded, and so I began packing up the equipment, and we made tentative plans to meet again at the next available opportunity. I shook Sam's hand. He gripped mine tightly and looked me in the eye,

"Was that alright, Ricky? Did I do okay?"

"Perfect Sam, you were perfect," I replied.

Chapter 7

Typhus Strikes

A few weeks after the first session, we met up again at Sam's flat. The first hints of spring were in the air and the sun was shining, but still Sam had the heating cranked up. Sam asked about my daughters again and we talked as I set the equipment up. I asked how he had been, but Robbie interrupted, "He won't tell you himself, but he's not been great." Sam shrugged his shoulders and waved his hand, "I'm alright, don't worry."

As we all settled into position, Sam out in front, with Robbie and I behind the camera, I could see Sam was immediately more at ease than he had been at the start of the last session. I knew though from Robbie's warning last time that there were some difficult moments ahead. Sam admitted he had no idea where we had finished off last time we met, and so I prompted him that we had been up to the early years of his time in the ghetto. I asked him to describe the room they lived in again. He thought for a moment and then began:

> All I remember is that it had one room, a bed, a settee, and a couple of chairs and a table. There were cooking facilities. I don't know what it was. It wasn't a proper kitchen or anything, but it had to all fit in one room. So, whatever it was, it wouldn't have been a lot. It would have been like a stove which probably in the winter kept us warm, and it allowed the cooking.

We weren't in there all day anyway. Most of the day we were working. When we came home from our work, we all sat down and somehow, under the circumstances, my mother prepared some dinner. We all ate and then went to bed. The following morning, we got up and we all went to work again. And that carried on for all the time we were in the ghetto. I'm talking about nearly four years.

Sam stopped for a moment, as if he had come to the end of his time in the ghetto. Robbie later explained to me that over the years, Sam had become used to telling his story in broad brushstrokes. Often when doing talks at schools, and only having an hour or so to talk, Sam would usually tell his story in the simple form of a series of chronological events. At the start of our sessions, he always needed some gentle encouragement to express the finer details of his story and his experiences. In this instance, I asked Sam what the food situation was like for them in the ghetto.

Well, in the morning, we had what was supposed to be like a breakfast. My mother would make a cup of coffee, and we had a piece of bread very similar to the size of what we got at lunch time at work. When we went to work, we didn't get anything until lunch time, which would be between one and two probably.

We all had ration cards, so we spent the entire amount on the card, and we also had ghetto Marks, which was ghetto money, but not German Marks. As a matter of fact, I had one. I don't know how I managed to get it. I put it away somewhere in the other room here and I tried to find it. I wanted to show you the ghetto Marks.

Then, if we had extra money, we would be able to buy black market food. There was a bit of that, but originally, it came in from outside the ghetto. Rumkowski was supposed to have organised all this, but a lot of the food got wasted for some reason or other, which as I was a kid I could not agree with. I don't think my parents could agree either, because some food was dumped, in the middle of the winter, outside, like vegetables and potatoes. And at twenty-five degrees of frost that would freeze, and by the time we got there, it was rotten and had to be thrown out. So, then we had used all our rations and that continued all the time. We were always hungry.

We had shops organised by the police. As a matter of fact, where we did the shopping with the ration cards, it was almost just outside our yard, so it wasn't far. My mother would go every few days, in the morning, before she went to work. She would get all the groceries, or whatever else, and it was all stamped on the card. I mean if there was one loaf of bread for a week, that was it. We wouldn't be able to get more unless you went on the black market, which I didn't know much about because I was too young. But my parents did bring back some food in the odd times after the rations were delivered, I remember that.

Robbie, who had heard much of the story before, at times, would learn new information that he'd never heard his dad talk about before. He would sometimes say "okay" and "really" as his dad talked, and then I knew that this was information that he was hearing for the first time too. When this happened, Robbie wanted to dig further into that revelation and try to uncover more stories or details that otherwise might have remained hidden. In this instance, Robbie asked his dad what they used to do for washing and cleaning.

I remember what there was in the room. It was a big dish, and we had to bring water in from outside; there were no taps like there are here. We had to bring buckets of water; it wasn't even warm, because we couldn't warm it, so she would put it in a big dish, and with a tea towel, or whatever, just wash us, wash our faces, our bodies.

I don't remember exactly about our clothes, but we had reasonably clean clothes, because my mother was looking after us, whether it was a proper wash or just a quick one, I don't know. We couldn't get the water heated, that was the problem, because just imagine to heat the water, you know, in the kettle, over the oven, and keep putting it into the dish. By the time we poured it into the basin, it wasn't hot anymore. So, they did their best. I don't think we were clean. Put it this way, there was a lot of disease going around because we weren't that clean. The clothes we had when we came into the ghetto were the same clothes we wore throughout our time there. I don't remember getting new clothes.

I started to get a real sense of the life Sam was leading in the ghetto. His memory was vivid and clear, and he spoke with such energy that it was difficult not to be right there with him. I asked him if he had begun to find out more about what was happening in the outside world.

Well, our parents were talking about it, but we were just kids initially. Maybe, later on, we started realising what was happening. Initially, we didn't know. We all knew that there was something going on and that's how we lived. We adapted to it. Those who adapted are still here like me; those who couldn't adapt, they went very quickly.

I think mentally, I felt that I had to adjust to any situation. But as I said, some people couldn't adapt. They went possibly from luxury to all of a sudden, ghetto life. I'll give you a typical example from 1942. There were a lot of transports coming in from Germany, Luxembourg and other countries that were occupied by the Germans, and these people came from a luxurious background, because they still had fur coats, and they had loads of food with them. These people died like flies. Within weeks, there were only about half of the initial immigrants who came in. So yes, it could have something to do with getting conditioned to the life. It's perhaps that I didn't come from such an affluent society that might have helped - but in reality, who knows. We don't know.

At times, hearing Sam describe his life so vividly, my mind wandered off attempting to recreate the scenes Sam described. I couldn't help but think about the world Sam talked about, but as clear as the descriptions themselves were, the concepts nevertheless seemed impossible for me to understand. I asked Sam how when the weeks were turning into months and then turning into years, did he just accept that this was his life forever?

> Yeah, towards the end, when we were more grown up, and maybe it was two years, three years into the ghetto, and I wasn't a kid anymore. You see, I went in at aged ten, so I would have been at a certain point getting on for fourteen towards the end. We did keep asking our parents about what was really happening, and we started absorbing it slowly, very slowly. We realised how the future was going to be. We didn't look too far ahead because we didn't know whether we were going to be in the ghetto forever. Then, we started to hear that we would be transported to different camps. We didn't know that we were going to a place called Auschwitz-Birkenau, but just to a different place, which as the Jewish police explained to us, was not like the working camps.

> As I got to that age, you know, maybe twelve to thirteen, then we knew that any transport leaving in the ghetto was going to Chelmo, and the people in the transport would be exterminated, especially the kids. Children were being taken away in transports, and they were gassed, sometimes on the way there. Initially, they had gas, you know, which they killed

people before they got there, and then they just buried them in a multiple burial.

On numerous occasions, Sam would admit to me that he simply didn't know about something. He would say he was a child and from within the ghetto, he couldn't have known about this or that. However, some of the stories Sam described contained details that seemed to contradict that sentiment. I asked Sam if some of his memories had become mixed up and if certain things he spoke of came from information he learned after the war.

I think initially, the rumours came from the Jewish police, and maybe some of them would have come from the ghetto inhabitants as people talked to each other and so on, but it wasn't anything definite. We learned after the war what Chelmo really was.

Towards the end, I got to know more, but they were rumours; there weren't any positive things. Even when I got to the camp at Birkenau, I could only see what was happening there, but I didn't know either politically or in general, what was going to happen to us. After the war, in most cases, I learned what had actually happened. I was a child. We didn't know and it's very difficult to explain how I really felt. Imagine you were me, you know. But most of the time in the ghetto, we were like zombies.

Robbie had an understanding of the story that I didn't have, and at times, he would steer his dad back towards a subject when he realised that Sam had skipped some details. At this point, Robbie asked Sam to discuss what he remembered about the notorious speeches that Rumkowski had made in the ghetto.

> Yes, I remember. Basically, he said that the order had been given to send so many elderly people out from the hospitals, and he had to do it, although he found it very difficult. But if he didn't do it, the Germans would come in and they might do it worse. And whether we believed it or not, I don't know. The same was with the children when he got an order to send many children out. He made another speech, warning us, you know, what might happen if he didn't get so many children out from the ghetto; that the Germans would come in and they'll do it themselves and it would be much worse. And what really happened was we waited until the Germans came in, and they did, on one occasion, I don't know whether I already mentioned it. A truck came in, two trucks actually. We were all waiting there, and they raided apartments and picked up children from infant age to about four or five, and just threw them through the windows into the trucks. Some of the children were already dead by the time they got into the trucks. So, the Germans did it themselves.

> We could not understand Rumkowski properly. As I grew towards a certain age in the ghetto, I didn't agree with Rumkowski. I didn't know much about it, but I didn't agree. I didn't know him, but from what we heard from before the war, he was a very prominent man in the Jewish community, a man

well aged already, grey hair, slight beard and yeah, he did a lot of good especially for children, but he changed when he had an order from the general from outside the ghetto. His name was Biebow, the general who co-ordinated the whole ghetto and passed all the laws to Rumkowski to carry out. Whether he did carry them out because he wanted to do so, or for his own survival, we don't know. I think until the end of the ghetto, most people couldn't understand Rumkowski's policies.

I think he liked the power, because he was living like a king. He was dressed well and had all his brothers around. He lived a life of luxury, until the end. With the last transport, he also went to Auschwitz, and from what we were told, he went straight to the crematorium with his family. But I don't think that anyone knew really why he did what he did. Okay, I'm not saying he could have done his job, you know, better for us, but a little bit better than he did. Like I said, to bring in food and allow it to go bad before people had consumed it, you know, that wasn't normal, it had to be deliberate.

I think at this point, Robbie realised that Sam was avoiding a topic that was going to be difficult for him to talk about. In the very kindest and gentlest way, Robbie asked Sam to explain how Grandpa had died, Sam's father. Sam looked down at his hands and took a deep breath. His face hardened, as I imagine all the painful memories flooded back. He looked at Robbie, then to me:

It was very hard because he was the head of the family. It's difficult really to get my memory back to the exact situation. He had typhus and he must have been in bed, or in the room we had, for several days. So, I don't think he went to work maybe, for almost a week. And when he passed away, obviously we mourned for so many weeks, until we got used to life without him, which we had to. We saw him being poorly, so we realised that he was ill, but I didn't know he was going to die. I can't speak for the rest of the family.

I don't really remember reacting to it in the way I would have acted under normal circumstances at home, because I was hardened to it already. Mum was working very hard. I remember her crying for days. And she would say to us that we've got to be strong because our father had passed away.

Sam lifted his glasses away from his eyes, there were tears there, but he blinked them away and replaced the glasses on the bridge of his nose. I didn't want to push Sam further here, and when I looked at Robbie, he didn't say anything either, and so I asked Sam how the conditions changed in the ghetto as time went on.

The conditions changed for the worst. Every day was worse than before. Walking through the ghetto, there were more dead bodies, people were screaming, dying. In general, the conditions were terrible. It is again so hard to explain what really happened, but day by day, the situation became worse and worse for us, and we became more hungry, thinner and hardly able to walk. The sanitary conditions in the streets, I mean the toilets we had to go to, were communal toilets for the whole block of flats. They were absolutely disgusting. The smells were awful and nothing was cleaned properly. They had cleaners, but I wouldn't think regular daily or weekly ones. It was when it would get really very, very dirty, and very smelly, only then, they would decide to clean it. Who even organised it? We don't know. Well, I don't know.

I asked if Sam sensed things were changing.

Well, until the end, we didn't know. It's only maybe days before that we were told that we were going on to a different camp, and the transport from the ghetto was allocated only so many people each day. Eventually, we were allocated when to be marched out by the Jewish police. So, we were almost the last ones, which could have been several weeks from the beginning of people leaving the ghetto. When we left, it was the last transport. There were still a few thousand people, but I think we were one of the last.

I wondered if Sam new the specific date. For example, did Sam know when it was his birthday or even what day it was?

No, but we were asking all the time in the ghetto. You didn't know whether you had been in there months or years. It just became one big day. We heard from the grownups, the year and so on, but we did not know exactly, day by day. Although, before the war, we were not that orthodox, but we kept all the Jewish religious holidays. However, in the ghetto, we did not even know the days of the religion, like New Year or Yom Kippur.

I asked Sam if people kept up their religious practice.

There were sections that did, but not all of us did. They created a Shtiebel but I don't know how they managed to save the Torah and all the Jewish books. I have no idea, but they created this situation, and it looked like a shul. Before the war, the Germans raided the Shtiebel, and those raids continued throughout the duration of the ghetto. But how long they survived, I don't know. I know there were several like that. I remember my father's routine after work on Shabbos. He would go to Shul, because he would work on the Sabbath, the same as any other day. There were some people that did believe in God and that whatever happened was God's will, which they still say now. I wouldn't say I am a strong faith believer, but it's something to cling onto. So, I think we all had this type of mentality. We didn't have faith in religion or God, but there was something in it, and I think most of it was the way we were brought up. When I go to Shul on Yom Kippur now, I think I do it for my parents, not for me.

Anyway, we found out only days before that we were going to leave. I don't remember exactly how many days, but there would be a few days warning beforehand. Don't forget there wasn't much to take because we had no possessions of our own, from our own home anyway. But, I remember my mother put a few things in a bag, like in a pillowcase, to take with us. That was to be the end of our time in the ghetto. We had no idea where we were going to go to next.

Chapter 8

There was no Goodbye

Sam took this natural conclusion of his time in the ghetto to reach for a drink of his water, and I used the moment to try and process all the things that Sam had just described. Because every day in the ghetto was the same, the same routine, same times, same room, same people, Sam had compressed almost four years of his life into about half an hour.

I thought about how important and informative the years of eleven to fourteen had been in my own life. In some ways, these had been the best years of my childhood. I was growing up, discovering music and girls, forming friendships that would last my entire life. For Sam though, these years had been ripped away from him. He had been forced into hard, manual labour, and living in depravity and filth. Food was scarce and often rotten. Dead bodies left to rot in the streets were as common as traffic lights are to us now. His father had also died in the middle of all this, and he hadn't been allowed the dignity of a proper burial. Instead, Sam was forced to carry on as normal, no time to grieve; he had no choice. Actually, he did have one choice - do what you were told or die.

I looked at Sam while he gently sipped on his water, perched on the edge of his sofa. He looked petite and fragile, his arm quivering as he lifted the glass to his mouth. A drip of water ran out of the side of his mouth and down his cheek. He quickly wiped it away with his other hand. I thought about how this delicate old man could possibly also be this brave young boy that he described. What must it have felt like to have lived through these things and to carry them with you through the decades?

I was becoming mesmerised by this incredible man and his story, as it unfolded. However, I also felt anxious about what he might tell me happened next, because watching this adorable, sweet man's heart break as he relived his childhood was not an easy sight to watch. As if on cue, he looked at me and smiled. I know now that this smile was his gentle way of saying 'are you ready?'

> We were given the order by the Jewish police that we were to march to Radegast station. We would be going by train but we didn't get a description of what type, just that we would go by train to other camps. They came to co-ordinate the marches, and they came to tell us in the apartments when we had to move out, so they gave us some time, but only two hours, maybe three hours. I don't know.

> So, we marched from our home to Radegast station, and I didn't know what to think about whether we were going to survive. Were we going to get killed? Then, we stopped thinking about anything. We were just walking like zombies. We didn't talk to each other. I walked with my brother, sister and mother, and we didn't even talk to each other. When we got to the station, there was chaos.

> I remember that I was wearing my normal clothes, a pair of trousers which I had the whole time during the ghetto, and a shirt. It was summer, in July, which

was the middle of the hot weather. I didn't carry anything. I know my mother put certain things in a pillowcase, but I don't know what she had packed. It must have been something she treasured, so she was carrying it, and my elder brother was helping her. But there was no discussion. We were all somehow bemused with all of this. We didn't do anything of our own will. We just walked like zombies; we had to. If we didn't walk, we would get killed. Although it was the Jewish police, if we tried to stay back, they would force us back into the queues to walk to the station. I think it was about two hours. It was a long walk. We probably didn't eat anything because we hadn't been to work, so we didn't get anything there, and whatever we had was from some food we put in the bag that my mother prepared. I don't know what that was.

Don't forget, they had still over a hundred thousand people living in the ghetto, before the liquidation. So, there would have been thousands. Yeah, maybe two or three thousand. There must have been because I remember when we arrived at the station, there were screams and shouting from people everywhere. We didn't see a train, a proper train, just these cattle wagons, and people were helping others to get in them but some of them didn't want to go. They were not in a hurry because they thought that maybe if there was no room, they would be sent back into the ghetto. So, they would have already known where they were going. Some of us pushed ourselves towards the cattle wagons, thinking maybe we would get a better place inside. It was absolutely chaotic, but the German police made sure that everybody on the ramps was put into the trains. Nobody was left to go back to the ghetto. We were absolutely crammed in. There were probably a hundred people in each one of those cattle wagons, and we were stuck there for hours without water, toilets, or anything. It was probably about twenty-eight degrees, and they shut the doors. There was no air and people were already collapsing. We ended up lying on top of each other, and it seemed like this went on for hours. It was hours before we even moved. People were screaming, "Help, help, help" but nobody was in a position to help. When they stopped screaming, we realised they were dead, and we ended up lying on top of them.

This was the journey from Lodz ghetto to a place unknown at the time to us. I remember it took maybe a couple of days, maybe longer. We arrived and the doors opened. It was night-time; what time of night, I don't know. So, the Sonderkommandos and the Kapos and German police shouted, "Alle Raus, Alle Raus," meaning, "Everybody out, everybody out." Those of us who were still capable of getting off on their own left, and we also left the dead people there. I remember seeing the Sonderkommandos coming to drag the dead out into a wagon and wheel them away. We didn't know exactly at the time where to, but we know now that it was straight to the crematorium.

We saw the German police with the guns and dogs were barking like mad. There were bright lights shining on us, because it was dark. But we started getting frightened, although we were conditioned to all sorts of terrible situations by then. But we saw the German police there, and the way they were acting, the Sonderkommandos, dragging out the dead people; it was a shock to us. As we were standing on the ramp, the next command came, you know the story, men on one side, women on the other side, so we had to do that. My mother and my sister went on one side, me and my brother went on the other side.

Sam stopped to take a deep breath. Robbie quietly reassured his dad that it was alright and to take his time. I sensed from Robbie's gentle tone of voice that he too was sad, but he tentatively encouraged his dad on by asking questions, "Dad, did your mum get hold of you? Did she give you a kiss, give you a cuddle or anything? Did she say something to you?"

Sam tried to get the words out:

No, there wasn't time for it.

He broke down but somehow, continued:

This is something that ...

His eyes filled with tears, his lips trembled, he struggled to speak. Robbie started to get up, "Take your time dad if it's hard for you."

This is something that bothers me.

Sam choked on the words as they came out:

Because there was no goodbye.

Sam cried, breathless, smothered sobs. Robbie went over, sat on the arm of the sofa and put his arm around his dad's shoulders. He gently planted a kiss on the top of Sam's head, "It's alright. Take your time dad. It's alright."

They stayed together like that for a few minutes, and then Sam gathered his composure and he nodded to me that he was ready to go on. Robbie headed back to his own chair, sighing as he crossed the room.

Me and my brother stayed on one side, and my mother and my sister were forced to go to the other side. But there was no goodbye. We didn't know the situation or what this meant, so I didn't get a chance to say goodbye to my sister, to my mum.

I think we were taken before the women. We left them on the ramp, when we were taken to Birkenau. Also, when I was waiting on the ramp with my brother, I saw a German soldier throwing a sweet or something to a five-year-old girl and as she bent down to pick it up, he shot her dead, and then as the mother crouched down to her child, the mother got shot too. And, although obviously, it shook us, bad as it was, we were already partly conditioned to it, and I don't think it did that much to us anymore. We weren't living in the real world, in real conditions, or in real situations. It was just something that was happening and all I remember saying, and I think that I kept that saying in my mind the whole war, 'Thank God it's not me'. When I saw people being hung, people being shot, 'Thank God it's not me'. I don't know how my brother felt as there was no discussion between us.

So, it was night-time when we were marched and It must have been hours after that it started getting light already. We were marched to a place called Birkenau. We knew that's where we were because when we got off the train, the Sonderkommandos shouted at us, "Alle Raus, you're now in Birkenau in a working camp."

I was with my brother. He was older than me, bigger than me, tougher than me. I held his hand. All I remember when we got into the camp in Birkenau, when we saw the conditions, I said, "We will never survive." He said, "Oh don't worry, we will survive," all in Yiddish of course, "We will survive, we'll see Mum and Sala very, very soon." He tried to give me hope, whether he meant it or not, I don't know. And that's how we marched, and when we got in, further into Birkenau, we were allocated into a big building.

As we walked in, we immediately saw the dirt, and although it was in the middle of the summer, it was all wet, and there were bodies lying everywhere. We looked on this side, on that side, and that's when I turned to my brother and said, "We'll never survive."

We entered into a single-story building, very long with an elevated gangway in the middle. We were put to one side and others were put onto the other side, and we had to lie down. It was all concrete. There was no bedding or anything. We had to lie down like herrings, head on one side and the other person with the head at the other side. This was still early, early in the morning, and I remember a Kapo walking on the gangway, and he was shouting to us that anybody with gold teeth in their mouth had to report it because otherwise the Germans would rip them out. I don't know how many did have them, because there were a lot of rich Jews that had gold teeth before the war. Anyway, we stayed there for several hours until it was morning, and I remember we got a black coffee. There was a trolley coming with a Kapo, not a German. He had a trolley with coffee and bread, and we were all given this piece, it was like that (he motioned the shape of a tiny piece), and I remember this like it was today, my brother said, "Here you have half of mine."

Sam broke down again. He held his hand out to demonstrate how his brother had offered him the bread. His hand was shaking uncontrollably as he tried to speak. The words didn't come out.

He took a deep breath and tried again:

I said no, but he tried to keep me alive. You see him there.

Sam pointed to the photo on the mantelpiece. Looking at the picture of his brother sent Sam into despair. He couldn't get his words out again. He was crying deeply now and struggled for breath:

> I'm sorry. I'm sorry. Anyway, we stayed there in that building until about, maybe lunchtime. When we got up, we were all asked to go to be counted, so we had to stand in the line, outside the block and they counted us all. After they counted us, we were free to go. Sometimes though, we had to wait because if they didn't tally how many people there should have been in that room, they had to find the people who were dead in order to account for them.

> Once everyone was accounted for, we were free to go around Birkenau. We were walking around, and we already saw the chimneys, because we saw the smoke, and this is where the rumours were getting around, that this is where the crematoria were situated. But we still didn't take it in, what it was. What is the crematorium? What is Auschwitz and who goes there? You know, we didn't think we were going to go there, and that carried on for several weeks. It was the same routine every day. Get up, roll call and then you had the day to just wander around. It repeated itself, the same thing as when we got in, every day.

The telephone rang loudly and it jolted us all into the present moment. It felt abrupt too, like waking up from a dream, or in this case, a nightmare. Sam's story had both Robbie and I totally enthralled, and it was a strange sensation to emerge from that world back into the real world, like the lights going on in the middle of a film at the cinema. Robbie answered the phone and wandered around the room talking to the person on the other end. He paced up and down while he spoke. Sam was quiet, watching Robbie and listening attentively, in case his input was needed.

I took a moment to gather my thoughts. There were just so many questions in my mind: Why did this happen? How could this happen? How was it kept hidden?

I understood that there were no answers, though.

Chapter 9

Just called by our Number

Robbie finished on the phone and relayed the conversation back to Sam. It was some arrangements for a doctor's appointment. Sam nodded. "Where were we up to Ricky?" he asked me.

"You had just been talking about your brother offering you his food portion, and then being stuck in the same routine at Birkenau," I reminded him.

> Okay, yes. Let me see. We knew we couldn't go to the wire fence because we also knew we couldn't escape, because it was electrified. We learned that because other people might have made that mistake, and might have got killed, so we knew it. But, we could smell the stench already, you know of the dead people, so we had some idea. My brother tried to explain to me what a gas chamber was, that it was where people were gassed and cremated. So, obviously, he already knew more than I did. He was four years older, but I couldn't absorb it.

> After several weeks, maybe three or four, it wasn't too long, maybe just a fortnight, the Germans came and picked my brother up to take him to another camp. And I remember we sat on a stone, both my brother and I, and he held my hand, and he tried for me to go with him to the camp. I was crying. I wanted to go with him, and the Germans separated us. You know, they took him away, and I was left on my own, and I never saw him again.

The way I felt was like I had been dumped in a big ocean without a life belt, that would be the exact feeling that I felt. I walked around on my own, in tears, crying.

Two days later, we were assembled again, and we had to queue up for our number to be tattooed, which, for me, was B7965 (Sam showed his left forearm). It's still on my arm. Once I had the number, there was no name, I wasn't called Szmulek, or Sam, or Gontarz; just a number, B7965. Right through to the end of the war, I was just called by the number. So were all the other inmates.

I asked Sam what happened exactly when he was tattooed.

I think it was just one guy doing the numbers. I remember the room was only a small room, probably half the size of this. We were outside in a big queue. It was the German police actually controlling things. It was a German who tattooed you, so all you did was stretch your arm out, you know, then they pulled your arm halfway towards them, and from what I remember, this thing that looked like a pen, I didn't know what it was, and he just didn't look at you. Hang on, there was another person, and he was writing, and he was taking your name. That's right. So, they knew the name to each number. They had records. That's how they got to record everything, but we weren't called anymore by the name, I only know now that there was a register of the number with our name. Then we were known by the number only. But whenever we did talk a little bit to one another, we introduced each other by name not by number. The only people that used the number was the German authorities. When they called us out for anything, they'd use the number. They called me seven nine six five.

There was no work to do in Birkenau. To me, it was like a transit camp. There might have been some work, maybe there were factories, but don't forget, every time a transport came in, they were allocated to different blocks and different situations, whether for some people to work, or to just stay there and look at the atrocities that were being committed.

Until we left, I was in the block from when I first came in, the one with the gangway in the middle. We went to sleep every night in that place, and as I said, we had to sleep on the concrete. We didn't have any clothes to put under our heads to make a pillow. So, we got conditioned to it. I don't know how. I don't even know how we ever slept or we fell asleep, and woke up, fell asleep, woke up during the night. All we heard was screaming, people dying and screaming for help, "Help, help, help" and nobody bothered even to try to help. We got into a situation that we just couldn't be bothered helping anybody else when we couldn't even help ourselves. That carried on for another couple of weeks or so, maybe. I can't put an exact time because it would be very, very difficult and I might not be accurate with the times.

I was interested to know if Sam and the other prisoners actually did anything or if they just stayed in the hut.

No, we had to get outside because we had to be counted. We had to assemble every morning at a certain time. We didn't know the time; we had no watches. It could have been six o'clock in the morning, because it was summer don't forget, so it was light in the morning. It could have been six or seven. There was no time for us in any case, you know, and then, we were just walking free within the camp. We saw dead bodies all over the place. Those dead bodies became the norm, even from the ghetto already, because the ghetto was like that all the time, not as bad as Birkenau though. Birkenau was an absolute shithole.

Well, the conditions were worse because we were in a camp rather than in the ghetto. In the ghetto, we were still living in humane conditions because we lived in an apartment, and we also went to work, and although we passed the dead bodies, it still felt like freedom. When we were in Birkenau, it wasn't the same feeling, it wasn't freedom anymore. We were interned in a camp and thinking, 'What is going to happen next?' So emotionally, we already had a feeling about what was coming to us.

Toilets were the next aspect of life in Birkenau that came to my mind. I asked Sam about the facilities.

There were public toilets inside, probably twenty toilets, you know one next to each other, which was for all the inmates, not just for one block. There were queues also, because don't forget, even if there were, I guess, twenty cubicles, there were thousands in Birkenau, so we had to queue. When it was your turn, you had a cubicle, and it wasn't separated. It was open, just a hole in the ground. There were twenty holes. We were sat one person on one side of you; another person on the other side.

Once we were in the barracks at night, we weren't allowed to go to the toilet. It would have been in the summer so it would have been about eight o'clock, nine o'clock because the evenings were still light. Luckily, because we were young, we still had a reasonable bladder, not like we have now, and we could hold it. Don't forget, we didn't drink much anyway, we didn't eat much, so we didn't use the toilet facilities normally anyway. Our whole system changed. We became much thinner, you know. If you look at the documentaries, we were all walking around like skinny zombies. That's how I was; that's how we all were.

I wondered how much talking took place as the day unfolded.

There was somehow a silence between the inmates. Very, very little conversation took place amongst us. I think we were all subdued by the conditions we were experiencing. We had to endure these terrible, terrible conditions, although we got used to them, but they became worse every day, practically. That's why you had so many people dying. They didn't die from being shot by the Germans or being hit, they died of the conditions. They couldn't take it anymore. It was the same when we were marching on the death march from one camp to another. We all walked but some of them, even though physically, they might have been able to walk, they couldn't take it anymore, and so just deliberately left the march. We marched like five together in a row. So, one of the five could just walk out of the line because he knew already he would get shot, because as we walked along, we could see dead bodies, the people who had been shot before. In Birkenau, we were like zombies. We spoke very, very little. Maybe there were times we would talk a little to each other. There would be certain questions you would ask, maybe where somebody was from, and one would say from Lodz, from Hungary, from France and so on, and that's where we would finish. We wouldn't get into a conversation.

Soldiers came in and did pick out some of us, and just enjoyed hitting us and treating us terribly. The Kapos consisted of Poles or Jews from every country that Germany occupied. They were hostile. There were different stories about the Kapos: some people say that they were helped by the Kapos. I don't remember during the whole war getting involved with any German, or Kapo, or Jewish policeman that I could talk to, and who was trying to help me or being civilised with me. I never had that.

The conditions were very depressing. Knowledge started to come about what was happening, because we saw the smoke. And as I remember, just walking backwards and forwards, sitting on our own, meeting somebody and having a few words. There was nothing to talk about. It wasn't normal life. You meet people in normal life and say, "Well, what you doing tonight?" There wasn't such a thing. Anyway, we knew what we were doing - nothing. That was Birkenau. Since the end of the war, I have heard that there where factories; I didn't know. There was supposed to have been factories in Birkenau that people worked for the Germans. I don't know. I'd never been to a factory, had never seen a factory there. I never worked.

All we kept saying to ourselves was, "Tomorrow liberation, tomorrow." We heard planes. We didn't know who they were, whether they were English, American, or Germans. We didn't know who was who. Every time we heard a plane, we thought the war was going to end: "Tomorrow, liberation."

That was July 1944. Probably, I was there for just about four weeks from July to September or October 1944, maybe. You see this is where I'm stuck with times, and I think most survivors are the same, we don't know the times or the dates.

Sam shrugged his shoulders. I looked at Robbie and we both knew it was time to call it a day. It had been a harrowing session for Sam, and he looked tired.

Since the conversation had begun a couple of hours before, Sam had gone from a young boy living with his family in the Lodz ghetto, to becoming a fourteen-year-old left all alone in Auschwitz-Birkenau, the section in the overall Auschwitz camp complex where most of the extermination of Jews took place (and the worst location from that perspective in the whole German concentration camp system). Also, he had lost everybody he loved.

There wasn't much conversation as I packed up my equipment. Sam was quiet and contemplative. Robbie too. Sam suddenly came to life again, "Ricky I've got a copy of a little book I made a few years ago, I'd like you to have it. It's not a proper book but it tells you about my life and there are some pictures. Robbie, can you go get it for me please?"

Robbie disappeared out of the room but returned moments later with a hardback blue book and he handed it to me. I said thank you and told Sam I would read it later. I finished packing away the camera equipment and tucked the book into my bag. I reached out for Sam's hand and said thank you again to him. As he shook my hand to say goodbye, he looked at me and said, "No, thank you Ricky."

***

I had promised myself that I wouldn't do any outside research while I was listening to Sam tell me his story, but when he handed me his book, I considered this to be part of Sam's ongoing dialogue.

The book was hard-backed, and landscape oriented with a shiny, light blue cover. On the front cover was a small photograph of Sam smiling. It was just a head and shoulders shot but you could see that he was smartly dressed with a shirt, tie and jacket. Sam's age was always hard to place, throughout all the different stages of his life depicted in photographs, but if I had to hazard a guess, I would say he was about twenty-five years old on the cover of the book. Underneath the picture were just four words in a bold, lowercase white font, *let me tell you*.

The title made me laugh; it was very Sam. He was saying, 'let me tell you' in both the simplest form of just 'let me tell you a story', and I also imagined him saying it with his Polish accent, shoulders raised and gesticulating with his hands 'let ME tell YOU'.

The book was beautifully put together. There were more pictures than words, some of the pictures weren't of Sam or his family and were just historical images, no doubt taken from the internet and most likely without permission. These images generally depicted such things as maps of Lodz and Poland, images of the Birkenau camp, the German cavalry and Chaim Rumkowski during his notorious address to the Jews in the ghetto, which Sam had already described to me.

As I turned the pages further into the book, I came across a picture of Sam's family. The picture showed the five members of the family - Sam, his mum, dad, brother and sister - and had a caption which said it was taken in 1931. It was a formal family shot, clearly taken in a photographic studio with a strangely picturesque, obviously painted, outdoor backdrop behind them. Sam was probably about two or three years old in the picture, and he looked tiny perched on his dad's knee. Sam looked cute with shoulder-length, black hair, and a severely cropped fringe across his forehead; he was holding a ball and looking distractedly off camera. I stared at the picture and tears came to my eye. I felt an actual physical pain. I have only met one of the five people in the photograph, but as I looked at them all sat together, a beautiful, ordinary, happy, family posing together in a photo studio, I couldn't help but cry for what I know that fate had in store for them.

I looked closer at the face of Sam's father, Avrum, dressed in a suit and looking so proud to be surrounded by his young family. I found myself picking up my phone and looking at a picture of me, sat with my wife and two daughters on a recent holiday. I was that proud dad, just like Avrum. I thought for a while about how none of us really know what fate lies before us, and yet how much we take for granted. I looked back at Avrum and his family and then again at me and mine. I vowed to myself to try to be as present as possible as much of the time. Life is precious. We can never know.

We all make these promises to ourselves in the key emotional moments of our lives, but it's actually living it out consistently that the true value of these lessons really matters.

I closed the book and put it away.

I couldn't look at it anymore.

Chapter 10

Waiting to Die

It was a few weeks before we were able to meet up again. Sam had been really poorly and in and out of hospital after developing an infection following one of his dialysis treatments. Robbie kept me regularly updated and I checked in with him every few days to see how Sam was doing. Sam had been administered antibiotics intravenously in one of the major hospitals on the other side of the city. He had responded well to the medication and so had been recuperating at his home for a few days by the time we eventually met up.

Robbie met me at the door, as usual, and helped me in with the equipment. "He scared the living daylights out of me these last few weeks, Ricky," he said as we moved into the communal hallway of the block of flats, "I was seriously worried for a while." I clenched my teeth and took an inward breath. "Exactly," Robbie said, clearly understanding my wordless response.

As we entered the corridor to the flat, from the lounge I heard Sam say, "Oh Ricky's here." This made me smile. When I entered the room, Sam was sat in his usual place on the couch and was as bright and animated as I've ever seen him. He made fun of my beard which I had lazily allowed to grow beyond its usual stubbled form. Sam was from a generation where shaving was something you did every day, like brushing your teeth. It wasn't something you choose not to do. His generation were also always remarkably well turned out, just as Sam was every time I saw him; he always had a crisply ironed shirt, a smart pair of trousers and often a sleeveless cardigan neatly buttoned up. On this day, as it was coming into spring, he had a brown and beige, chequered, short-sleeved shirt and a pair of matching brown braces.

We were all very relaxed with each other by now, and Sam told me about his recent time in hospital while I set the equipment up. He was a lot more nonchalant about his recent illness than Robbie was, swatting it aside like nothing more than a slight irritation.

As it had been a while since we met up I reminded him that in the last session, we had come to the end of his time in Auschwitz-Birkenau (Auschwitz II). Relaxed with the entire process now, Sam picked up seamlessly from where we had finished off:

Leaving Birkenau, we were marched out, because where we were going was not far. The soldiers came and assembled us. That was without notice. They didn't need to give us notice and they marched us to Auschwitz. What we've seen on the way is the chimneys. We did have some idea of what had been happening there, but that is now confirmed to us, what really was going on there.

From what I remember, it may not be accurate to the minute, but I think it was a half an hour walk. Don't forget we didn't have watches, and being the age I was, time really didn't mean anything to me. I never had a watch even before the war, you know, so if I had to guess, I would say it was a half an hour walk to Auschwitz.

As we walked, there was a road, an asphalt road, not dirt, asphalt. Auschwitz, like I might have said, was very neat and clean. Even the barracks were very, very clean. We didn't actually recognise a crematorium. We didn't know what it was, but we saw the chimneys and we saw the smoke, and we smelled the smoke but we already halfway knew what was happening.

And you must realise that; I think I mentioned it in the previous interview, that we were conditioned to it all because we expected the worst anyway, especially once we got to know that people were killed in the gas chambers. We already knew that my mother and sister, they were separated from us, and they went into Auschwitz separately. We knew what might have happened to them, although my brother told me that we'll meet up together with them. But I think that was just to give me hope, and I think he wasn't a stupid boy; he realised a lot more than he told me, maybe just to keep me calm.

We know now that it is likely that Sam's mother and sister were taken to be killed in Auschwitz-Birkenau within hours of their arrival from the Lodz ghetto. Sam continued his story:

As we crossed from Birkenau into Auschwitz, there were just big gates. We left big gates, and we marched in to more big gates, which you often see on the films now, you know, and we were walked up to a block, number thirteen. This is my first block which was a children's block.

So, one thing about Auschwitz, as I have mentioned, it was always neat and clean. It wasn't like the ghetto.

We walked all the adults and children together, but what they did was they separated us and when they walked up to block thirteen, which was the first block we came to, they called all the kids who were to go into that block, by our numbers. We didn't know what was going to happen or what we were going to do. We went in and we saw these bunk beds, although they weren't bunk beds as we know them now. They were wide enough for eight people and they were three tiers high. So, what we did initially was we sat down, we didn't lie down, and we weren't allocated space or specific beds. Well, there were no beds, but we had to pick a bunk. It was all wood, like floorboards, in each block. I would say over a hundred people in each room, because they were very big bunk beds. But if you imagine between eight or ten lying on the bunks and three tiers, and it's quite a long way back, they were along the barracks, as far as you could see.

We were then told what we were doing. We were given a job to build a brick wall up to a certain height. And the following day, we did that. We built up this wall and then in the afternoon, late afternoon, we all lay down and there wasn't anything else to do. We got our coffee and piece of bread, and we lay down on the boards and just messed about that afternoon. There was nothing to do.

Every day, there was a different Kapo, with a stick and he would hit us whenever he felt like it, for no reason other than the excuse that one brick or another that we had laid wasn't straight enough and so we had to take it off and put it back again. This repeated itself every day. As soon as we built the wall, the Kapos knocked it down again. It wasn't a wall for use, it was just being used to make us work.

When we finished in the evening, we got another cup of coffee and a piece of bread and that was it for the night, but the bread was only about that size, you know. (Sam motioned a small amount between his forefinger and thumb). And we stayed there doing nothing, we just sat, we didn't lie, we just sat like that (Sam sat up and shuffled himself on the edge of the couch with slumped shoulders and a solemn look on his face).

Some people were talking to each other if they knew each other, and now and again, a Kapo would come in, not a German soldier, could be a Polish Kapo, or a Jewish Kapo and they would start kicking or hitting us for no reason, and that evidently went on in every barrack.

I imagined that it was impossible to sleep in such an environment. I asked Sam about it.

We didn't sleep in the night. I think we fell asleep more from tiredness and the things that we've gone through during the day more than normal sleep. There were many, many times we woke up and we didn't know where we were, and lying on the hard block of the boards, it took a few seconds to realise where we were. Actually, I don't remember being cold in the barracks, but people were screaming all the time. You heard them, "Help, help, help me." This was going on right through the night. People died during the night. People died.

Sam looked at me and Robbie and shook his head:

People died while we tried to sleep and there was nothing we could do.

He paused for a little while the thought hung in the air. I looked over at Robbie and he gave me one of his looks of disbelief that we had already shared many times. We formed an unspoken language, the two of us. Just a look and we knew what each other was thinking. We often didn't want to interrupt Sam and whatever he was feeling at that moment, allowing him the space to feel it fully. I came to learn from Robbie that a lot of what Sam was telling me was likely to be the first time that Sam had ever actually said it out loud since it happened. I became acutely aware of this, and I learnt to be comfortable within some of the most uncomfortable silences I have ever experienced, but I knew it was important to allow Sam to be there with it. Eventually, Sam would let us know he was ready to speak again. It could be a simple nod or a gentle smile, and then he would turn to me, and I would know it was okay to move on.

I asked him to describe the children's block and the surrounding areas.

I do remember that it was like a stone building whereas the others were wooden barracks, and it had the number thirteen on the wall. I've heard it said since then, but I honestly don't remember, that there was an upstairs. Whether it was just a ground floor where we worked in one section and the bedding was in another section, I can't answer that truthfully. Honestly, I can't remember.

We had no way of getting out, of walking out or looking out. At this stage, it wasn't that bad. It was clean. It wasn't the worst. I seem to think it was maybe October 1944, I'd have to say I was in the children's block for a few weeks, maybe a month. Then, they picked out some of the numbers. Well, some German soldier would come in, whether a Gestapo or an ordinary soldier, I can't remember, and from a list, he would call out numbers, where each number was another boy. We had no names then you know, and we came forward and then he marched us to another block.

We just walked, just followed orders, like zombies. You didn't really think, 'Oh well, am I going to be happy here? Oh, that is nice. That is awful.'

I didn't take it in, the scenery. It didn't matter to us for some reason or another. I mean, we were subjected to conditions and told to do what we were asked and so we just did it. So, when you went to different places, new places, you didn't really take much notice. You asked me before about the ghetto and did I remember details like the wallpaper in the room, but you didn't take notice of these things.

The other block, I'll be frank with you, I don't remember that really either. I was in two other blocks. If I went there, I think I'd be able to find them and pinpoint where I was, but I don't remember the number of the blocks. Now those were bigger blocks and the bunk beds there were the same, three floors high and no bedding, just boards. What people did, I didn't do. We had these clothes, these striped clothes on, and some people took the jacket off and they cuddled it up and put it underneath their head like a pillow. But not many of us did that really because there was a lot of thieving going on. So if you did that and all of a sudden, somebody pulled it out, you've got no jacket and no pillow, you know.

Our normal clothes were taken away; we were just given somebody else's. They could have been the trousers either too long or too short, whatever. So, we got striped clothes actually when we first got into the kids block, and from there, I had those clothes right until walking out of Auschwitz.

When we got into the main blocks - adults and children together, we had orders from Kapos, because in Auschwitz, most of the orders and the directives came from Kapos. "You are now in Auschwitz labour camp and you will have to do the work as we tell you," they told us. We just looked around, we didn't know what to do. This was early in the morning, even though there wasn't much to do that morning. We still got the coffee and bread and we just sat down, and different Kapos came in and shouted at us. They started beating us for nothing.

When we got into the adult barracks, we just picked somewhere to sleep. There were obviously some people already there, grown-ups, but we had to pick our own place. I remember I picked the ground floor, the first floor, you know, because I was small and I didn't feel like climbing, but I managed to find room. When you were with the grown-ups, the inmates seemed to be kinder than the kids when we were in the Maura Shula - the kids block, frankly because I think the grownups looked at us as children and they did try to help us. There wasn't much they could do, but whatever they could do to help us, I think they did it.

So, now we were allocated different jobs. One job I had, I walked outside with a German soldier, out of the camp with a big stick and I picked up paper or leaves or whatever there was, and then I put it in the bag, and that took a couple of hours. Then, he brought me back, brought me through the gates again, into the block where I was, and by then, it was nearly time for lunch. So, we had lunch in the afternoon, and after that, I was just lying about doing nothing, lying, sitting and so on. That's what everybody else was doing.

I remember walking out. As a matter of fact, I remember walking out of there the first time and I had terrible trouble finding the way back. You had to get back to the right block, because if you went into any other block, they would throw you out if they didn't know who you were and where you should be. It took me a while, but I walked around and there was some grass verges; it looked actually nice and clean. Auschwitz was a clean camp. When I got back, I just sat around in the barrack doing nothing. There were thin crowds of people walking around outside. There weren't a lot of people. Some were walking from one block to another but there wasn't really much difference to see, because don't forget, in Auschwitz, each block was the same. So, wherever you walked, you'd have passed quite a wide path of grass. It wasn't a clean patch of grass but there was a grass verge, you know, which looked a lot neater than from my memory of the ghetto.

You must remember that after four years being incarcerated in the ghetto and experiencing all the different atrocities we had been going through and witnessing, we were conditioned to it. All we wanted was to survive. We kept thinking to ourselves, 'Tomorrow the liberation, tomorrow the liberation.' If we saw a fatality, even in Auschwitz, there weren't that many dead bodies lying around like there were in the ghetto, but any dead bodies we saw we said, "Thank God it wasn't me," that's what we kept repeating all the time, "Thank God it wasn't me." Whether that helped us or not, I don't know.

They were so organised and tidy by now at Auschwitz that they almost got it like a factory, but instead of producing things they were just killing people. They improved how fast, how much time it took to kill people, and that's what they did. We knew partly what was going on but we didn't know exactly. It wasn't explained to us. We didn't read it, but we imagined, we had seen the chimneys, we smelled the smell, so we knew that those people were being burned. Well, I mean, I don't think we had any official knowledge from anybody about what was going on in the camp, but we knew.

The other job I had, that wasn't a good job, was for the first few weeks I was placed somewhere called the suszarnia, which is actually a Polish name, it's not a German name. I was surprised that they didn't change the name, suszyc is Polish, you would interpret as being a drying room. Suszyc is to dry. Our job, one I did for quite a long time actually, too long, was to sit on like a table and I had to climb up on the table with crossed legs and stick the souls onto the German soldiers' boots. And we used this solution, which was so strong, so deadly that a lot of people died, and they had to keep bringing more people in after the others had died from the smell, you know. I was there for several weeks.

That happened every morning, after the Appell, the name call, because I've not told you much about the

Appell yet. While I was in the barracks, before we went out to work, we had to assemble for an Appell, and we would stand in rows of five. As we were counted, the soldiers would pass us with a big stick, look at us and just point at whoever they fancied, and that person had to walk out and he was taken away. We knew then that he was taken to the gas chamber.

Robbie bristled at this statement, shifting noisily in his chair, and breathing loudly. He leant forward and asked Sam if there was a system to the picking, or if they just picked out the weakest ones.

I don't think so, you know, because I was weak and I was small and somehow, I was ignored, so I don't know honestly. I don't know how or why; I think it's just they had the freedom of doing everything. Don't forget, they did whatever they wanted. So they would go down the line looking and pointing … no … yes … no … maybe they counted to ten, maybe they counted to five. I don't know. It was very difficult for us to know that, but once, he pointed to you or put the stick on to your chest, you had to walk out with him. He put several aside, because he picked out a few, so you would walk out and stand beside him waiting, but you knew your fate. There was nowhere to run because you didn't want to get electrocuted by the fences. So, you stood there, there could have been half a dozen and then he marched them away from us. And this is when we realised that they would go to the gas chambers. That happened every morning while I was in Auschwitz. We all wet ourselves when he passed us,

literally wet ourselves, but we just, we just waited
to die. It wasn't a question that we thought we were
going to die, we were waiting to die. It was just
something that I don't think that anyone outside of
the survivors can even think or imagine; that we
waited to die. It was like it was a thing to come, you
just didn't know when.

It was becoming increasingly difficult to hear
these words coming out of Sam's mouth. I would look
over at Robbie and he would be either looking up at
the ceiling, and shaking his head, or leaning forward
with his head in his hands.

I asked Sam if dying was something that he
actually wished for, that death would be an end to the
suffering?

Many times I wished for it, Ricky. I wished for it in
Birkenau. That was the first time I wished for it. It's
very difficult to express how it was when you were
in big groups and you know, you think you're going
to die and yet you still follow orders. Resigned is the
word, not scared. Was today my day? Yeah, you are
just resigned to whenever it happens. I think we
passed the stage of being scared. Even getting hit
was just one of those things; they came in and they
hit you. People were crying obviously because when
you got hit with a stick, it hurt and you cried. You
didn't want to cry but by this stage, you had lost
everything; you had nothing to live for, but the
struggle for life was to survive and tell the stories.

I was quite surprised by this. In the midst of everything he was going through, at such a young age, Sam actually considered survival in order to share his story. I remembered reading Viktor Frankl's incredible book, *Man's Search For Meaning*, where Frankl (another Holocaust survivor) had also articulated the key to his survival as holding on to something bigger than himself, something beyond his own personal struggle, and that was the idea of sharing his story and helping humanity as a whole. It seemed a grand and surprising gesture in the middle of such chaos, and especially for Sam who was potentially only fourteen years old at the time. I asked him if that was actually something he consciously remembered thinking about?

> Yes, definitely. I'm gonna get out of here and I'm going to tell my story. It helped me. Absolutely. Well, my family too. I thought about them and hoped to see them again. Really though, I would only have hope for my sister because I didn't know where she was at the time, and for my brother, but I didn't know where he was at the time either. I had it already in my mind that my mother would have been taken straight to the gas chambers and the crematorium in Birkenau, because that's where most of the women went straight away. So you did think you'd meet up with part of your family at least and that did help. It gave you something, because you wanted to give up on the death march when you walked and you wanted to walk out, but you knew you'd get shot and put in the ravine somewhere, so then you thought no, maybe you

would survive, and there was a chance, so that thought came to me on many occasions.

I asked Sam if he noticed that some people also had that same sense of hope he had and maybe they survived because of it.

I don't know many people who thought the same way as I did and survived, or how many people died by not believing. That's just the way I thought. I don't know, because it's only the survivors that I spoke to after the war. None of them really knew exactly why they survived. We often ask ourselves the question - Why me? Why not him? We don't know. If I don't know about my own family. Why me? Why not my brother? You know, it's a question that we can't even ask. We can ask, but we can't answer ourselves. I don't know, but going back to while we were there, there were people who gave up yes, and they definitely went straight away to death. And there were people like me, who hoped and hoped, and hoped. But even I experienced many times when I wanted to give up, but something stopped me. And I kept going.

Chapter 11

My Landsman

Often when Sam said something powerful and poignant, his words would hang in the air for a moment or two. Neither Robbie nor I wanted to be the one to break the reverie of what had been said. Sam himself, would often ponder the words that had come out of his own mouth, staring off into space, as if the words had come from somewhere deep inside of him, and he too, often seemed surprised at their potency.

I noticed Sam's eyes shift back towards me and then to Robbie. So I took the opportunity to ask him to tell me a bit more about the work he had described doing.

> I had those two jobs mainly. I don't remember any others. I remember walking in the camp, once I got used to it. After I'd walked during the day several times, I'd walk in the evening, but after a certain time, which might have been eight o'clock in the summer, it was all quiet. There was nobody walking. The odd sound you heard, was when you passed a barrack and you heard somebody screaming or shouting for help. You heard people shouting help all the time.

I asked Sam if he made any friends at all in the camps, or was that a silly question?

I only met one boy that I struck up with, and that was Genek, who was also from Lodz. We became very, very friendly, but even then, with Genek, we didn't talk much. He was in the kids block with me actually, where we met and became friends. Initially, we exchanged some conversation like where we both lived and where we went to school but after that we just had thoughts of our own, and we would walk together, wherever possible but often in silence.

Moving out from the kids block, he was with me all the time, thank God, and so we managed to stay friends almost to the end, to the liberation. I think now that he would probably have been sent over from Birkenau at the same time as me too, but we just hadn't met yet.

Robbie interrupted at this point and told me a story:

You won't believe this Ricky, but a few years back, we sent off for all the registration documents and anything we could, any documents to help trace my dad's journey, and unbelievably, when coming out of Lodz, Genek's name was about five names away from my dad on the list, and then, the same when they went into Birkenau, so that's how they were in such close connection.

Sam nodded in agreement:

You see, when we entered block thirteen, the children's block, I don't know how many boys were there. It was like a constant movement of kids, but when we went there, there weren't any boys from previous times. It was empty. The previous kids would have already been taken out. So, we might have been maybe a hundred kids and Genek was amongst them. We sort of edged together during the time that we were there, maybe not initially or immediately, but over the time, we became very, very good friends. He was the only one that was from Lodz, from my town and somehow, it meant a lot if you met someone who was, what we call a 'Landsman', someone from your own town.

But you know Ricky, the strange thing is although we might have spoken some words at first, I don't remember having a conversation really. It sounds strange I know, but the only time we had a proper conversation was after the liberation when we were in the displaced persons camps. Then, we talked to each other about my home, about his home, what we did, and we became very, very close. We were close in Auschwitz, but we became much closer after Auschwitz and the liberation, because he helped me, I helped him and that served the purpose of us being together. To have him there, it gave me a better feeling, a good feeling, but that feeling seemed only temporary because we constantly felt as if we were both awaiting death.

Every day, when we would go off to the jobs, we never knew whether the other one would return later in the day. One-time, Genek didn't come back for several days. I got really worried. It brought me almost to tears because I didn't know what happened. It worried me, and I became distressed. When I talk about it, even now I feel it.

So then, the next thing happened in January 1945. I can't tell you the exact date, like I said, we didn't have dates, all we knew was that it was light or dark, day or night. One morning after the Appell, we were joined with another block, and we had to join with another block again, and we didn't even know exactly what was happening and then another block would have joined us until the queue became miles long, you know, and then we realised that we were being marched out of Auschwitz. We didn't know where we were going or what was going to happen or if it was the end of the war because we still saw German soldiers guarding us. So, we knew that we weren't liberated yet.

Chapter 12

Nights Out in Manchester

One evening, when I was catching up with Robbie on a video call, we got talking about going out in Manchester city centre. Decades past our heyday, and now in our late forties, we giggled as we reminisced about some of the big nights out we'd had in our youth, and how the thought of those heavy nights sent shivers down our spines now. Robbie started telling me a story about his dad:

As kids, I'd say when I was sort of sixteen going on towards seventeen, we used to go to the Playpen on Bootle Street in Manchester, and it was one of those places, because we were underage, it was very hit and miss on the weekends whether you'd get in or not. But, once you had brokered the door three or four times and they knew you, then there wasn't much of a problem. But initially, until you'd got past that door the first few times, it was always difficult.

Manchester, at the time in the late 1980s, was a very, very vibrant city, and so my dad was always out on the town at the same time, because him and my mum had split up. He was then living in Whitefield and mum was living in Broughton Park. My dad was living his life as full as he could and with his newly found freedom, he had become a bit of a face around town. He knew loads of people from all different walks of life, whether they were immigrants coming to the UK or whether they were English people; he had pals all over the place. You could literally get in the car and go somewhere, even out of town, and you would bump into somebody who knew Sammy G, wherever we went.

Well, in Manchester, because we were at that young age, there was only a couple of places that we could even look at potentially trying to get into, because we knew we wouldn't get in to all the other places. But there was a brand-new nightclub that had opened up on Deansgate in Manchester and it was called Richfields. All the faces in Manchester used to go there, all the well-to-do people. It was the cream of the crop in Manchester. They used to hold the Miss Manchester competitions there and various things like that. And I said to my dad one night, just jokingly, "What's that new club like?" And he was raving about it and so I asked him to get me a couple of membership cards, and without even considering the age or anything like that, he said he would.

Anyway, lo and behold, he used to go to Manchester city centre on a Wednesday night, Thursday night, and a Saturday night, and so when he was out that night, he got me two silver memberships for Richfields. I was gobsmacked.

Anyway, the following weekend, me and my mate went out and bought some new clothes. I think I bought a new pair of trousers and a shirt because we were thinking we'll go into Richfields regardless of where any of our mates were going.

So, we rock up to this nightclub, two little sixteen-year-old kids, dressed to the nines, and these two massive bouncers in black suits looked down on us and said, "Where do you think you're going?" I confidently said, "We're members, alright?" And I showed him our membership cards. The guys look at the cards and he said, "Where did you get these from?" So, I replied, "Off my dad. You probably know him, Sammy G, little guy with long white hair." The guys immediately stepped aside and opened the door for us to let us in. Dad had pulled a rabbit out of the hat for me. He was so well known around town.

As things went on and I became a little bit older, when I was eighteen, the Hacienda in Manchester was in full swing. It was 1989, 1990 and we were legally allowed to go out in town, and the Hacienda was my haunt. It was just a brand-new scene. The music was different. The people that were coming out were all different and it was fabulous.

But with dad being a man about town, he used to often frequent various different places in Manchester because he'd go into his usual haunts, which were Richfields, Lloyds and places like that, and then he'd often do a bit of a tour of other night clubs after that. Now, I love my dad very much, and I'm proud that he was having a great time with all his friends but I said to him, "You do know that the Hacienda is out of bounds."

And he looked at me and said, "What do you mean?" I said, "It's not for you; it's my place." And he said to me straight away, "No problem."

But to be honest, because Manchester is a small city, we ran in to each other quite a lot, and my pals would run into him a lot. He was living his life the best he could, and I was so happy to see him doing that.

Happy times. On the left is Sala next to Sam's mum, Ruchla. Srulek, Sam's older brother is in the middle, whilst Sam sits on the knee of his dad, Avrum.

Top: From left to right: Sam's father, Avrum; his sister Sala; his mum, Ruchla; Sam aged about nine years old; Sam's brother, Srulek; and Uncle Icrek. Bottom Left: Sala. Bottom Right: Genek who gave this picture to Sam before Sam came to England.

Top: Sam in bed at Villa Park, 1946.
Bottom: Sam with his friend, Avrum, at
Feldafing displaced persons camp in 1946.

Top: Sam and Genek on Lake Starnberger, 1946.
Bottom: Sam, Genek and Guretz, one of the older
boys who befriended Sam and Genek after their
liberation, swim in Lake Starnberger. This image is
the original of the one featured on the book's cover.

Above: Sam and Guretz after rescuing Genek
who almost drowned in Lake Starnberger.

Above: Sam and Genek snowballing outside
Villa Park, the house that General Eisenhower
enabled them to live in near Feldafing
after the liberation.

Above: Sam on a bike, not long after
he arrived in Manchester in 1947.

Top left and right: Sam, in Lodz, 2019, outside where he and his family lived before the Germans invaded.
Bottom left: Sam, in 2019, outside Auschwitz 1.
Bottom right: Sam outside the children's block 13 where he spent time when he was in Auschwitz.

Top left: The tunnel into the Lodz apartment block
Sam and his family lived in during his childhood.
Top right: The forecourt of the block. Sam and his
family lived in one window on the first floor.
Bottom: In 2019, Sam returned to the station at
Auschwitz, the place where he last saw his mother.

Top: Robbie, Adrian, and Sam in Lodz after visiting
the camps and the locations of Sam's childhood.
Bottom: From left to right – Robbie's son, Remi; Sam;
Robbie's wife, Clare; Robbie's daughter, Lucia.
Family meant everything to Sam.

Top: Sam and Sheila, out for a
family meal in Manchester.
Bottom left: Remi, Sam, and Lucia.
Bottom right: Robbie and Sam.

Top: Rik (the author), Sam, and Hayley (who did her dissertation on Sam) at the big family meal in 2019. Bottom: Sam in Lodz, in 2019 in the square where as a child he was banned for being Jewish. This photo beamed out to the room from the screens above Robbie when he made his speech.

Chapter 13

Packed in like Herrings

Sam was now going to talk about the next phase of his incarceration. He would be moving from probably the best known of the extermination camps to a lesser known one, although equally appalling as far as its conditions and its purpose.

> Once we went out through the camp gates, we realised that we were marching to another camp. We heard bombs falling as we walked. We didn't know at the time whether they were Russian, American, French or even German. We also heard a lot of shooting as we marched. This was when the death marches of Auschwitz started.
>
> They took thousands out of the camp and we marched for a day and a half. We stopped over in a farm somewhere, and we slept through the night. We stayed in the hay and we were guarded by the Germans who had taken us out of the camp. The next morning, we started again. Eventually, we got to a railway station very similar to the one we left from in Lodz, only much smaller. Again, they had cattle-wagons waiting for us, the same as in Lodz. They got us in there, locked us up and we started to move. I don't know how long it took but the train kept going for hours and hours. Finally, we got to a place, which at the time we didn't know, until we

actually got off the train and we saw the name: Melk.

I remember that when we marched, we didn't have proper shoes at all, so our feet were sore and painful. We still had on those striped clothes. When we got to Melk, it was cold. They got us out of the cattle wagons, assembled us and sent us in for delousing which took place in showers. We were frightened to go to the showers because we heard rumours about what happened there. We got undressed and stood in the shower petrified. We thought we were going to die there. We had waited for death to come but this time, we actually had a shower, a proper shower, thank God. The relief was so great. Then, they got us out again, assembled us and counted us.

Oh yes, I remember, they gave us a vest, just a vest to put on and I remember it was cold; we put our feet down on ice. And they counted us. There were a few dead. So we had to stay until they found the dead in the shower room or wherever they died. While we were counted, we waited. Then, they put us into the barracks.

The barracks were very similar to what we had experienced before. There were bunk beds, three high I think, but we didn't do anything. There was no work for us. We were there only about two weeks. There were thousands of us, thousands. I don't know how many there would have been in the blocks; they were a bit smaller than in Auschwitz, whether it was one hundred or one hundred and twenty, I don't know. I saw the numbers after the war, but at the time, we didn't know.

Melk, seemed to be smaller than Auschwitz, even smaller than Birkenau, but they managed to force the thousands that marched, all in there. After several weeks, they marched us out from there again. We didn't know this at the time, but what I found out after the war, was that by then, Auschwitz had been liberated on the 27th of January 1945. Those who stayed there, were liberated six months before I was. So, they were lucky.

In Melk, in the morning, we did the roll call again. We had already had our coffee. We had to have our own container. If we lost it or if somebody stole it from you, then you wouldn't get a coffee. So, we always had that in our hand and we got a coffee and a piece of bread. After that, we just walked around; there was nothing to do. We didn't know if there were any gas chambers at the time. But I did read after the war, there was a gas chamber there, but I didn't see it.

There were buildings all the way around, very similar to each other, all about the same size as the one I was in. It was all cemented; there were proper buildings painted in grey. There was just dirt, though; there was no grass. There were electric fences, and a tower block where two soldiers with machine guns looked down at everyone all the time. If anyone tried to get out, they would be shot straight away, something that we witnessed.

This was now the third camp Sam had been in in a short period of time. He discussed moving from one to the next almost nonchalantly. I understood how desensitised he had become but I wondered what he thought all the movement was about, and why they didn't just keep people at Auschwitz and kill them there?

We didn't really know. You must realise that after all our experiences, we just followed orders - where, what and how to do things. And if we didn't do as we were told, we were hit, shot or whatever. We didn't think. Outside people, like you and Robbie and thousands of others, can't imagine how we thought. We didn't think about why they did it. We had stopped thinking like that a long time ago.

For example, after a few weeks in Melk, we started marching again. We didn't know why or where, we just did it, and soon, we arrived at the station. When we marched out from Melk, all I can remember is that our thoughts were that we were going to another camp, because we already had experience from the ghetto to Birkenau, from Birkenau to Auschwitz, from Auschwitz to Melk, so we thought that we knew we were going to another camp, but we didn't know where. I seemed to think that they evacuated everyone from Melk at that time because everybody moved out. I learnt afterwards they did that because as the Russians neared one camp, they took us all out to another.

I don't think we even went to a station from Melk. Yes that's right. I don't think it was far because it only took several hours. We got to a place called Gunskirchen, which was another camp very similar to Melk; the conditions, the surroundings, the blocks were very, very similar. We went through an iron gate to get into it, and we were then allocated a block to go in. The bunk beds were the same, the treatment by the guards of being beaten all the time and shouted at continued as well.

I was struck by Sam's ability to remember names of places. I asked him if he remembered the names at the time or learned them afterwards?

I just kept them in my head because when we went in them, the first thing the Kapos would do was assemble us and tell us the name of the place. "You are now in your new camp, Gunskirchen and this is your labour camp," they would tell us. But there was no work, no labour, which we couldn't understand because to us, it seemed like a quarantine, you know, until we got to another camp. After a few weeks in Gunskirchen, we were again assembled in lines and marched out, and we hit a station where we were huddled into the cattle-wagons again.

We stayed there and that was very, very cold. Even though we were all inside, we were still freezing. People were lying on top of each other because they tried to get us all in, hundreds of people on top of one another in each cattle truck.

Eventually, we moved but we didn't know where we were going. Genek was with me all the time. He helped me to get on to the wagon. Although he was the same age, he was a bit bigger than me. We lost each other because once we started moving, you know, we didn't have a seat to sit on and we held on to anything. We were just packed in like herrings, so I did lose him for a while, but then, on the way out, I caught up with him again.

We travelled for several hours across Austria because that's where we were by then. We arrived at the next stop and all I remember was the snow. It was freezing; it was snowing like mad. They opened the doors and shouted, "Alle, Raus." All we had on was the striped jacket and torn shoes. Some of them had hats and some didn't. We assembled outside until everybody was out. Don't forget, there were several carriages, probably, about ten with several thousand people inside. We looked at the soldiers and they were dressed in fur coats, big boots, big, fur hats. We looked at where we needed to go and it was like a steep mountain. They walked us up. To walk up that mountain in our condition was too much for some and people died before they even got there; they froze to death.

Chapter 14

Dragging Rocks up the Mountain

After moving to his third camp, Sam was about to tell us about a fourth. These camps were a mere example of the hundreds of concentration camps in a system which the Nazis had created through the 1930s and used as an instrument of their vile regime as the war played out.

> We didn't know where we were going. I didn't know that Mauthausen existed, I had never heard of the place. This was now sometime in the morning, but we didn't really look around us; we were just walking and doing what we were asked to do. Don't forget, there were dozens of soldiers. I don't know where they came from but all of a sudden, there were dozens of soldiers and Gestapo with guns. The dogs were barking. The soldiers were shouting, "Schnell, Schnell," meaning, "faster, faster." It was chaos. So, we marched as much as we could, and it was very steep. When we got on top of the hill, all we saw was those big gates again. Mauthausen was like a stone fort, and you saw the guards on the towers. There were always two guards on each side of the tower. As we were marching, they had guns trained on us, in case anyone tried to escape. We couldn't escape though; there was no way to do so. Physically, we weren't capable of it, but they had the guns pointed at us anyway to frighten us, because if we looked up, we could see them. They tried to put the fear into us, but as I said, we didn't

even have any feeling anymore. Ironically, they weakened the fear actually because we were used to it.

When we got into the camp, I don't remember seeing barracks. All I remember was that we got to a place where we all lined up, and we were asked to undress as we were going down to delousing before we even went into a block or anything.

So again, we had a shower, and we prepared to die. But thankfully, it wasn't our time, for whatever reason. After the shower, we didn't get a towel to dry ourselves, we just got a vest like in Melk. We emerged from there freezing, and I don't know how any of us survived. Some of them did fall onto the ground and just died, but they were still counted. The Germans had to get the full count of how many went in and how many managed to get out. You see, the Germans were always very accurate in these things, very organised.

We were shivering like this (Sam motioned hugging himself and rubbing his arms). We were freezing. We just had a vest on. The temperature must have been about twenty-five below. We had an Appell, which was always outside. Time-wise, I can't give you exactly, but to us, it seemed to be a hell of a long time. This place looked different to the other places. It was very different, very disorganised, very dirty. Apart from the people who now just fell and died, there were also bodies all over the place, you know. And we saw them actually, because it was early in the morning. They must have been Kapos who were moving the bodies, putting them on wagons, and I think they were probably taken to the crematorium.

We didn't get striped dress clothes by the way, in Mauthausen, just civilian clothes, but it must have been the other transport's clothes from people before us who had died. I remember having a pair of trousers. After a long time, we were allocated a barrack. I didn't see anything else, just a barrack. We were pushed in like herrings again and we cuddled each other, pushed our bodies together. That kept us warm, whether they did it deliberately or not, I don't know, but if not for that, we would have all frozen to death, and there were hundreds of us. So just imagine, it's impossible, I know, we were all naked apart from the vest and holding each other like that, and hundreds of us in a bunk.

We stayed there for several hours. I met Genek again. We had lost each other again in the showers. When we were walked out from there, I'm just trying to remember exactly where we went. This is important.

Sam paused for a minute to try and recall something. I could see that he was struggling with the recollection and becoming frustrated at himself. Eventually, he just waved his hand in resignation, sighed loudly, and carried on regardless:

When the Germans came in and separated us, they shouted "Raus, Raus," again and we went outside. They marched us into a block and gave us clothes which we put on. Then we were ordered to assemble again. This was the second time that morning. Probably less than half the people remained. The rest were dead already. So they counted us and it was all written down in the books you know. And then, they took us to another block.

The other block was very, very similar to the ones in Melk and Gunskirchen - just wooden boards; the width was very wide, I remember in Mauthausen, there were many more people to each bunk. Maybe about forty or sixty because it was very, very big - all boards, you know, and they never allocated you a place; you just had to grab one. I always tried to grab the lower bunk, the first one, so I didn't have to climb up. As I said, I was successful with that. Then the commanders came in while we were lying there and told us what to do. We had to get up again and put the boards straight, not that they weren't straight, but they had to get us to do something. I remember that they said in German, "This is where you are going to live for the next few weeks."

That day, we didn't do anything. We went to bed and then, first thing in the morning, we got up. Next, it was Appell again, and then they took us to work, and the work was down the mountain. To us, it looked like a mountain anyway. We walked down to the very same place where we arrived, across the road. It was like a quarry, you know, and that's where we went to work. This work consisted of digging for stones. We were given jackhammers to break up the stones. They gave us each one, and I was at that time already probably getting on for fifteen. With that hammer, we had to dig stones, and shovel them into a kind of wheelbarrow. Coming out from the quarry, it was also back up the hill, which was very, very difficult for us. And all they did, the soldiers, was stand behind us with whips, not sticks, whips and shouted, "Schnell, Schnell," and every time they shouted it, you took a faster step. You had to do it, but then you went back to walking more slowly when you thought it was safe to do so. You could only walk on a certain path, but some people couldn't, and they got shot straight away. I worked at this for several weeks. It was unbearable.

This story of the work in the quarry shocked me. I found myself speaking to Sam out loud about this. I said, "So you haven't eaten properly for over four years? You've been in and out of concentration camps for the last few months with just a tiny bit of bread and a little drink of coffee? It's freezing and snowing constantly, and you are asked to break rocks and lift heavy wheelbarrows full of rocks up and down a mountain for up to seven hours a day under duress?" Sam nodded while I ran through these questions. I wasn't so much asking as trying to process the information for myself, as if by saying it out loud, it might make more sense. Sam continued to nod as I asked the questions. He was acknowledging my horror at the shocking detail of his descriptions, but he was also questioning his own ability to have coped with it all. He interrupted me:

I don't know how I did it. I ask myself. I don't know. Once we got on the top and then unloaded the wheelbarrow, we tried to take some time because we thought, 'well, we're not going to rush back'. You know, we'll get a little breather. There were soldiers that watched us, but they shouted from above, "Go down, go down, quick, quick, Schnell, Schnell, Schnell." So, I had no chance to have a breather.

We must have been there all day. After the Appell and after getting coffee and bread, we were there until it was dark. I don't know the exact timings, but I would think until about eight o'clock. As I said, we didn't know time, we can only guess what it was.

We just looked for these stones and dumped them in big piles outside and every morning, when we returned, there were less of them. So, they must have been taken away by lorries.

Robbie interrupted at this point:

The quarries were a special kind of quarry because it had a particular hard-stone and what the Germans were doing is they were using it a lot for their concrete to give it extra fortification.

Sam nodded his head:

I didn't know until after the war, when I started watching documentaries and YouTube, that these quarries were called Hitler's Secret Quarries, one's he used for military reasons.

This went on day by day, and then we went back to the barracks and we had a coffee and a piece of bread. The other thing I didn't explain to you about Mauthausen was the barracks, unlike Auschwitz or Birkenau, which was brick and cemented. In Mauthausen, they were huts and some of the huts were practically open to the outside. If you look at them now on YouTube, you'll see they weren't the same huts which were nice blocks like in Auschwitz, they were dirt. Anyway, we would go back to the barracks, and we were absolutely exhausted. That's why we slept.

Then in the morning, it was Appell, and the Kapos always came in and the first thing they said was, "Alle, Raus." They didn't wake us up properly. So, we all grabbed our bits of clothing and we went outside where we knew we had to assemble. We were counted and we walked down to the quarry again. Genek was with me and we always looked at each other and said to one another with just a look, 'Do what you've got to do'.

But some people just couldn't do it. They died. The way I see it was that it was a matter of adapting, and those of us who adapted, survived. If you couldn't adapt, you gave up, you didn't survive. That's why the minority survived, millions didn't. Not just Jews as many people often talk about, but millions of others too. They weren't all killed with the gas, some of them just died because they gave up.

There were times at Mauthausen where I wanted to give up, I did. The times when I couldn't wheel the barrow anymore and I was beaten with a whip and shouted at, "Schnell, Schnell." I felt like giving up, a lot. That's why when I managed to get on top of the mountain, I thought I would take a breather. I waited, but it wouldn't be allowed. That's why they had soldiers on top as well; to make sure that nobody took too long before they went back down.

You see the Germans, the guards, the SS, the Gestapo, all the Nazis, they seemed to enjoy doing what they did. It wasn't that it was forced onto them, or they were told to do it in order to survive. They enjoyed it. If I'm going back to when they raided the Shtiebel in Lodz and what they did in the Lodz ghetto when they threw the kids down, they didn't have to do that. They did not get orders from above. They did it, because after they'd done it, they enjoyed it. That's what they had been doing since their time in the Hitler Youth. They had got used to it.

Robbie leant forward in his chair and rested his elbows on his knees and his head in his hands. He sighed loudly and asked, "Dad, how did you not give up? Me and Ricky wouldn't have lasted a day on that mountain, let alone considering what you had already been through."

Sam shrugged his shoulders:

I don't know, just this thought that comes as you are fighting to survive, 'Maybe tomorrow, maybe tomorrow is the liberation'.

Robbie shook his head in disbelief. I was thinking the same thing as him. There is no way that either of us would have survived in those circumstances, not even for one single day.

Sam shrugged again. He had given the best answer he could come up with as to how he survived.

He continued:

In Mauthausen, we could see the planes and we heard bombs, but they weren't that near yet. We knew something was happening but we didn't know exactly what was going on.

The treatment of us after work, during work and before work was frightening because you were up against the Gestapo. There were all sorts of the Gestapo soldiers. They were all running around with machine guns, with all sorts of weapons and you know, they just kept hitting us for no reason or other. We were in no condition to resist. If anything touched us, we fell and if you fell to the ground in this kind of frost, you froze to death and some did, so, how can I explain it in one word? It was absolute, absolute hell.

Mauthausen was the worst of the suffering that we experienced by a long way. This was worse than in any other camp. Everyone felt it and it was very hard. The people were fighting to survive. There was some stealing still going on. For instance, if you lost your cup, you wouldn't get a drink. You'd steal one from somebody else. I didn't need to, thank God. I had my cup all the time. If you did not have a hat, you would steal one because you kept warm with one. Your cup, you kept it on you, tied to your waist. I had it on a string tied down to my jacket. The cup was banging away on your hip all day long when you were working, but we were used to it. It didn't really bother us.

The doorbell rang and Sam became distracted as Robbie got up to answer it. I took it as a signal that our time for this session was up, and while Sam seemed quite buoyant still, I was exhausted. I had found this session very difficult to process. Sitting in Sam's company and hearing him speak, calling on his memories and drudging them up possibly for the first time since they actually happened, was an incredible privilege to witness, although it was also very hard to hear. I couldn't help that my mind wandered, and I imagined the pain of this sweet, little fourteen-year-old boy. No family, all alone, starving, freezing. Working painful, hard labour, while all around him, people were dying. I imagined myself in that situation, and I couldn't help but feel that I would probably have been too weak to survive.

I bent down to give Sam a hug as I left. He said goodbye, and then contentedly, began playing with his iPad. Robbie walked me to the car. He talked a little, but I was quiet, my mind distracted.

This session stayed with me for the whole of the following week. I couldn't shake the image of these starving kids, in their striped rags, pounding up and down the hill lugging rocks in the freezing cold, snow falling, while the German soldiers shouted at them and hit them, forcing them to work relentlessly.

I hadn't heard about Mauthausen before that day, a place worse even than Auschwitz according to Sam. I had promised myself that I wouldn't research anything on the internet until I had heard Sam's full story as I didn't want to prejudice the story Sam was going to tell me, but in this instance, my curiosity got the better of me and I looked it up. I wish I hadn't now.

There is footage and images on YouTube that shows the prisoners marching up the steep hill with what appears to be boxes full of stone on their backs. They are crammed in close together as they shuffle up the incline of the side of the mountain. The footage I have seen is shot in what looks like a warmer climate than the snow and ice that Sam described, and it's unimaginable to consider how bad it must have been in the freezing cold, wearing thin rags and often, no shoes.

Since the war, Mauthausen has been converted into something more approachable, to allow visitors to go there but not to experience it exactly as it used to look. The steep mountain climb that the prisoners endured each day with kilograms of stone attached to their backs, is now a rather civilised set of stone steps surrounded by lush green foliage and plants. If you didn't know what it was you could be fooled in to believing it was an area of some natural beauty.

In one video I saw, a middle-aged man, in seemingly good health, attempt to simply walk up the stone steps at a leisurely pace. He struggles badly, huffing and puffing his way to the top. How can we even consider then the idea of thousands of underfed young men, already broken by years of abuse and the loss of their loved ones, being forced to climb that hill, under duress, for up to six hours a day, in freezing conditions without a break?

That entire week, these images and questions haunted me. I couldn't shake them from my mind. My dreams at night were filled with images of similar horrors, some of them directly from the things I had seen and heard; other images seemed to form from the darker realms of my imagination.

I did not sleep well that week.

Chapter 15

Don't eat the Soup

A few weeks passed before we were able to meet again due to an emergency in my family. Sadly, my time during this period was spent living a bedside vigil for my eighty-one-year-old father-in-law who was taken ill suddenly. Being in and out of the hospital for almost three weeks, and with my work-life taking a back seat, I had plenty of time to contemplate life, and unfortunately, death too. The time I got to spend with my family was dear and precious, but at the same time, my mind drifted to Sam and the way in which he was robbed of any opportunity for family life.

The unconditional love, support, care and attention which enveloped my father-in-law's last few weeks was jarring only in its contrast to the meaningless way in which life was extinguished casually in the world Sam grew up in. I had come to see in my own life how important and deep the grief at the loss of a loved one was, and yet death became a simple, matter of fact for Sam in the camps.

How had we, as human beings, drifted so far from our better natures that we could justify killing, hurting and maiming one another in the ways that we do? Spending time with Sam, and now facing a personal loss, had turned me deeper inwards. There were many unanswered questions that plagued me for a while during this time. I was keen to get back to uncovering Sam's story, perhaps I felt there were answers there for me as well as for him.

When I arrived back at Sam's flat after my prolonged absence, he was in great form. It was a gloriously sunny day ahead of the Easter weekend, but the heating was still on full inside the flat. We had a long chat about my recent family situation and Sam expressed his sadness to me about what I'd been going through. There was a warmth and sincerity in Sam, forged by his own life experiences, and so when he shared insights into the deeper worlds, you listened. His words soothed me, just the feeling of being with somebody who survived such trauma and tragedy was empowering and humbling. No matter what we might have been going through, it couldn't compare to what he had been through.

Amazingly, we picked up quite easily from where we left off, those last few days of Mauthausen.

> We never knew from one day to another when the last day in Mauthausen would be. We just got up in the morning for Appell and then we were told to line up, and we marched. That's how it ended there. We didn't know exactly what was happening or where we were going.

> This death march was very similar to the previous ones. We lined up in rows of five. We tried to hold on to each other. There was one soldier on one five, and another soldier on the five on the right. Anyone that got out of line was immediately shot and left on the side of the road. So, although you were marching, all the time, you saw the dead bodies of

people that had been shot. How long they had been there, I don't know.

We marched until we got to another railway station, and we were all packed into the cattle wagons again. I don't know exactly how long it took but I don't think it was very far from Mauthausen to Wels so it couldn't have taken that long, maybe a day.

Eventually, we arrived and they disembarked us. "Everybody out," they shouted. We were not at Wels yet. We didn't know it was going to be Wels, but we still had to march for about two or three hours until we got to the new camp. All we saw as we went in was that it was like a forest. There were empty sheds, you know, and we got to one big hall, like a shed with lots of straw, and we were asked to go inside. We didn't know why or what was going to happen. This was already in the evening, late in the evening. In fact, it was getting dark already as we walked towards the big hall, which was already getting full. People were lying on the floor and other people were on top of them, and I remember Genek pulling me back and he said, "Szmulek, don't go in there. We'll stay outside." So, he took me away. We were already guarded by the guards, you know. We couldn't escape. I followed his advice, and we ended up under a tree, lying down. We didn't have any covers or anything, but we were tired enough to fall asleep almost immediately. We were only there at Wels for about three or four weeks.

The food was very similar to the other camps in that we got a coffee in the morning, bread and water with soup for lunchtime, and then another piece of bread and coffee, black coffee or something, in the evening. But unknown to us, in the last week or two, the soup was being poisoned. We realised that many people were dying. We knew that over the period of the last six years, people were dying of hunger and all sorts of living conditions, but we didn't know why they were dying so quickly here, and we only found out after the liberation. We were told that they had been poisoning the food to try and kill people quicker because they didn't have other means to do so at that point. There were no gas chambers, for example. We didn't know what sort of poison it was.

All I remember is that I became very dazed. Aeroplanes were flying overhead, machine guns shooting, and it was all rush, rush, rush. We were drowsy and drifting in and out of sleep. I know now we had been poisoned, but back then, I didn't understand.

All of a sudden, we woke up, in and out of sleep and we found ourselves without guards, without anything. We didn't know why. We were liberated but we didn't know it. We were too poorly to know and although the very thing that we had been dreaming of for years was now a reality, we couldn't enjoy it because we were dazed.

All we knew was that there were no German soldiers around anymore and then the American soldiers arrived. When they saved us, they took us to a hospital where we were given medication. And over maybe a day or two, we became conscious again, and that's when we were told exactly what had been happening. And I was told that if the rescue had taken another day, I don't think that I would have survived or all the rest of us either. Thank God again that Genek was with me, and we then met up with some more of the survivors at the hospital. We became like four friends. Genek was from Lodz, the same town as me; another boy was from Belgium; and a fourth one was a Greek boy who was very funny.

Sam began to jump forward too fast, as if the craziness of the liberation still provoked a frenzy within him, but it was such an important time and I wanted him to share every detail, so I asked him to describe Wels.

There was a gate; there were no buildings like in the other camps. We didn't see a crematorium there or anything. It was just like a big farm with sheds, but what they did before we arrived there was to erect a wire fence and they locked the gate after we went through it. We never saw how big it was, but we didn't know much. I don't think we were really interested in that; it was already the last days of the long war. We just went there like sheep, you know; our brains couldn't take anymore.

We just sat around. Because we were dazed, I had very little awareness or understanding of what was happening. We weren't talking. I wasn't even talking to Genek. In fact, I was telling someone about this recently. I didn't realise that Genek and I didn't talk. It was only after he listened to my story that Robbie asked me, "By the way Dad, when you met Genek, what did you talk about?" that I had to think and my answer was, "We didn't talk." I honestly didn't realise that actually, until Robbie mentioned it. It didn't dawn on me that there was something not right with us not talking. But after you had asked "What's your name? Where did you come from?" then after that, there was nothing else to say.

I checked with Sam that chronologically, we were now in May or June of 1945.

We were nearly at the end of the war, in Wels. It must have been … I was liberated in May, so it would have been June.

I confirmed that there was nothing to do and Sam had been poisoned and was dazed. I asked him what else he remembered about the camp.

You wouldn't really say it was a camp. It was just a big farm, but we didn't see any animals. They obviously must have been taken away before they put us there, but I would imagine there would have been sheep and cows but it was nothing like that when we were there. It was still a hellhole but it was an empty environment. There weren't any buildings. There was nothing to do. We were just fenced in and guarded.

While we were there, we never went into that big shed. I think I forgot to tell you this but in the morning, we saw people coming out from the shed just walking about, and we found out from them telling us that half of them in there were dead, because they slept on top of each other. This is exactly what Genek had warned me about. It's why he pulled me out and why he didn't want me to go in.

And from there, we just walked about, sat down, or lay down. There wasn't any punishment anymore there because the guards didn't bother; they just tended to keep us in. But just before I became unconscious, we started to hear aeroplanes and gunshots that were getting nearer and nearer.

So, we were hoping, but we didn't bank on it because in the past we had heard this before, in Auschwitz or Birkenau, and it never happened. But we were hoping that this was the real thing. And by the time it did happen, I was already unconscious.

Chapter 16

You're Free Now

There are no adjectives to accurately describe what the six previous years had been like for young Sam. I've tried. Horrendous. Horrific. Tragic. They are just words. They just don't get close to the depths of the horrors that he witnessed himself. I watched Sam himself attempt to find the vocabulary to match his memories, but he failed, nonetheless.

It seemed that the bitterest irony of all is that when eventually, Sam did get to realise the freedom he had hoped and prayed for, and that seemed so impossibly unlikely and out of reach, he was poisoned, dazed and unable to realise it. I found myself shaking my head in disbelief at this irony. "So, one minute, you're slipping into unconsciousness and surrounded by German soldiers. And then what happened? Do you remember?"

> Well, there was a mix up. Maybe, I was not fully unconscious because I remembered the gunshots and then I woke up in a hospital and an American soldier in Yiddish said, "Bist Frie Nau," meaning, "You're free now."

> I still didn't believe it but after I opened my eyes. I started asking questions. I don't remember what I asked or what made me want to ask questions. It took some time, and I know they had given us some medication, liquid medication and when we came

around, which took a few hours, we felt a bit better. So they started giving us food and getting us up from our beds and sitting us down on chairs. Then, they started asking questions, and while some people might have been ready, I wasn't ready. I was still dazed; I still wasn't sure what was happening. My brain told me that we were being liberated, yes, but somehow, I couldn't believe it. It took time until I became a bit more normal in my brain to realise what was going on around me.

I asked Sam to describe how it felt to be there.

Well, the memories: we were comfortable with clean sheets, and beds which we hadn't had for the last eighteen months or so since we left the Ghetto, and yeah, it looked nice. I would imagine it must have been a German hospital which the Americans took over, and they were operating it to help make us better.

It was a big, big building, although don't forget, we're talking about seventy odd years ago, eighty years ago almost. It was a building very similar to a hospital now. There were nurses and American soldiers. The nurses took orders now from the Americans about what to do and how to treat us. I remember the nurses came over and talked in German to us. We understood a bit of German because Yiddish is very similar to the German, but we still didn't fully understand. If I go back in memory, I think it took me maybe a whole day to realise that we were really free and it was not a dream or a fairy tale or something, but it was the real thing.

I can't tell you how long we were in the hospital but it was certainly several days. We started getting food, but we didn't get too much. They knew that if they gave us too much, a lot of people had died because they grabbed and grabbed the food after not having anything for so long. So, I think they rationed what they gave us for the first few days, but what they did give us was good food, proper bread and proper soup and I think we got some meat and beans too. We started to eat more normally over the next few days. I don't know how many.

I wondered how Sam and the others had been treated; if the hospital staff were nice to them.

Oh, yeah, even the German nurses were nice because they had to be because they were under the Americans now, not the Nazis. I don't know what type of arrangement they had with the American soldiers, or how they operated with each other, but they worked together because it was the German nurses that brought the food to us. And this was actually very difficult for us to understand because before, we had always been shouted at by the Germans to "Raus," here and "Raus," there. All of a sudden, we were treated by the German nurses more or less in a civilised way.

The whole thing became very confused, not just for me, but probably for most of us. It took us several days to become half human. I felt that after what I'd gone through, even if this was the real thing and I had survived, that the damage I'd suffered could be permanent for me. That's what I felt.

What also happened when we were getting food and we sat at the table, because there was always plenty of bread, most of us, including me, grabbed it and put it underneath our trousers, storing it for later. We didn't believe that it would be the same tomorrow. Some of us over-ate and then became ill. We were half alert, not fully alert, to what was happening, because the whole thing seemed like a dream to us and we didn't know how to behave or what to think.

I imagined Sam had developed a huge mistrust of human beings.

That's quite true. We didn't trust anybody or anything and that's why probably our sense was to grab the food we couldn't eat and hide it. Plus, they didn't stop us because they knew - when I say they, I'm talking about the American soldiers - they knew exactly what had been happening and therefore, why we did what we did.

I think that I was in the hospital for more than just a few days. it might even have been even ten days, nearly two weeks. I also know that when we left the hospital, we were already in civilian clothes, so we must have been given these clothes to replace the striped jackets and trousers that we had worn in the camps.

So now, we looked more or less normal, but we were still very thin, all skin and bone most of us. We had no flesh on our bottoms, you know. I remember sitting on a chair even a soft one and it was very painful because I had no flesh on my bottom. The weight must have been half the normal weight for my age at the time.

I asked Sam to tell me about the ten days in the hospital. I wondered if he had met other children who had been liberated.

We started to talk, and we were opening up to each other, especially to Genek. I opened up a lot and I think it's the first time that I asked him about his family, where he lived and where he went to school.

Before, while we were in Auschwitz and on the marches from one camp to the other, all I knew about him was that he was from Lodz and he had been in the same places and the same ghetto as me, but I didn't know about his life before the war. So, we really introduced ourselves. Somehow, all of us opened up and talked like human beings to each other. I still can't understand the reason why we couldn't open up in the camps and why this happened after the liberation when we were free.

I assumed that this had been a coping mechanism, whereby if he and Genek talked about their previous lives while they were in the camps, it would have opened up a can of worms and made them deal with emotions and pain that wouldn't have helped, a point I shared with Sam.

I don't know. It's something that happened probably which doesn't happen to normal people. If you go on holiday, for instance and meet normal people, you ask questions about them, but this was something that you couldn't do in the camps. I don't know why, and I never even thought about it until Robbie mentioned it to me.

Anyway, this went on for ten days or something like that, you know, and then, we were given freedom. We made up a little group while we were in the hospital: there was Genek and the Greek boy and the boy from Belgium. So, we were four now. The other two were older than Genek and I, who were almost the same age. The other two were maybe four or five years older, so they were already men. We would have been fifteen going on sixteen.

Next, the Americans organised transport for us to go to the first displaced persons camp in Salzburg, Austria. Most of the boys went immediately into a big bus, but for some reason or other, the four of us didn't. I don't know whose idea it was, but we decided not to go with them but to make our own way and do our own thing. So we just walked out of the hospital. I don't remember who decided that we should do that as we weren't supposed to. Probably, it was the Greek boy because he was older. Regardless, we walked out of there, the four us. We were free. At last.

Chapter 17

Not Human Yet

As Sam described himself and his three friends walking out of the hospital into a world completely unrecognisable to the one he had last been free in, I too, felt a sense of elation. I could feel the tension fall away from my body, although I hadn't even realised how uptight I must have been prior to this. I could visualise the four of them taking those first tentative steps. In my imagination, based on Sam's description of the boys, I visualised them walking in size formation, tallest down to smallest. I wondered what you do first in that situation. Where do you go? What do you do? I didn't expect the answer I got when I put the question to Sam.

> We walked and walked. Quite soon, we saw a farm. We stopped to investigate. We saw a barn with a ladder going up to a higher floor, you know, with plenty of hay and straw so we thought we would just climb up there and see if there was any food or somewhere to rest. So, we all climbed up there and when we reached the top, we were shocked. There, laid neatly out on the floor, on some straw, was a German uniform, a gun, and a few army things. We realised that there was a Nazi there living in that farm.

> The Greek boy grabbed the gun, and I remember we waited until we saw somebody coming out from the

cottage, and it was a man. He was dressed as a civilian, but we thought that this was the one who the uniform belonged to, which was a Gestapo uniform by the way. So, as we went down the ladder to confront the man, the Greek boy pointed the gun at him and shouted, because we all spoke broken German or something. He told him to stay, and I remember the three of us had to tie the soldier to a tree with a rope, which we found in the hay. I didn't know what we were going to do; I just followed the other boys lead. But then from nowhere, the Greek boy shot him.

I was shocked and scared. The older boys ran off and so I followed them.

We didn't know exactly what was happening. Were we going to get caught or not? Maybe, by the time they would have been alerted, we would already be far away.

I also remember getting a bus to somewhere, only we didn't have any money yet, you know, so we just jumped from one bus to another, and we had somehow managed to get to Salzburg to find out where this displaced persons camp was. And very luckily, we didn't get caught. I would have thought that if we had got caught, it would have been by the Americans, which might not have been so bad, because the Germans had already lost.

I was visibly shocked at what Sam had just told me. I looked at Robbie. He clearly already knew the story because he shrugged his shoulders and tilted his head. It took me a minute to process the information - so many questions.

I asked Sam why the Greek kid had shot the man if he wasn't sure for definite that the guy was a Nazi soldier. Why had he done it?

He just didn't care. He ran back afterwards and told us later that he had stabbed him. I don't know if that bit was true. He was wild and angry and he had no sense of right or wrong.

You asked why he did it? Revenge. He took revenge. It wasn't a question of whether he was innocent or not, because even in the displaced persons camps, someone only had to point to someone and say, "He was a Kapo" and everybody fell on him to kill him, and that happened a lot.

How did Sam actually feel watching that all happen? Did he feel a sense of shame or achievement?

Achievement, because we strongly believed that it was the man who owned the Gestapo uniform. Why would a uniform of a civilian farmer, living there in a cottage, hide it on top of the straw in the barn? So, we had an idea, but whether he was or wasn't, I don't think it mattered to us. Don't forget, this was just a short time after we had been liberated. We weren't human yet.

The four of us kept together and it made my life much easier for me than if I would have been on my own. Once we got to the displaced persons camp at

Salzburg, we joined everybody else. We were registered as survivors.

It took several days organising the whole journey. What we called 'organising' in Yiddish actually meant stealing food from the farms. I remember Genek jumping through a window in a farmhouse, during the night and bringing out a big sausage like that (Sam motions a pulling movement with both is arms) and we had bags with us, you know, straw bags, and anything we managed to organise we put in these bags. Every now and again, when we stopped or we would eat, our only worry was that even though we were liberated, if we got caught by the Germans, they would send us back to the concentration camps because we didn't know how strong the Americans were. We were treated very, very well by the Americans, but we didn't have the security or belief in our own minds that we were really free.

We thought that it might be temporary, or just in a certain part of Germany. We didn't know that the war had really ended. Although the American soldiers told us in hospital that we were all free and the war was finished, we still couldn't believe it.

We managed to eat a lot better than in the camps obviously. We didn't have any money, but we just jumped on and off trams. I remember that we found out which train went to Salzburg, and we got on that train. When we got off, we didn't pay. Don't forget Germany was disrupted at this time, you know, and it only became more normal after several months.

Actually, it took more than several months. So, we ended up in Salzburg, and already, as we became more civilised, we mixed with everybody else, making friends, talking, and beginning to live a bit better, feeling better, looking better. We were still very skinny, and we needed to put a lot of flesh on our bodies, but we felt we were getting back to normal.

Next, I asked Sam if he had any sense of how he felt. Was he thinking about his family a lot?

Yeah, I thought about my family all the time. I knew, or guessed, that my mother wouldn't have survived because she was taken to the other side, where they went to the gas chambers and the crematorium. I didn't think that my sister survived, because my sister went with my mother to the other side. I didn't know anything about my brother, yet. So, I was hoping that I might meet up with him somewhere.

For several weeks, we didn't see any list of the survivors, you know, the lists that they put up so that people could check for any family members on there. But, when the lists were put up, I remember we all wanted to go to see them desperately in the hope of finding a surviving relative. There was a special office in Salzburg, where there were lots of lists with names of survivors. I looked for the name Gontarz. The day we got there, I was hopeful for some reason but when we checked all the lists, my relatives were not on them. So, I guessed that my brother hadn't survived. Remember, I told you what happened to him, we talked about it, at Birkenau.

He was taken away to another camp, and from then, I had never seen him.

I nodded my head to let Sam know I remembered. It was hard to forget that shocking moment when Sam's brother was taken away from him, and Sam was left all alone in the camp. I took a deep breath and tried to question Sam a little more about the displaced persons camp.

The camp was just wooden huts, but it was comfortable there. There were bunks, three high and we all were together the four of us. In the morning, we had an assembly room where we all went in and gave our names. I think they wanted to know who we were and to distribute the names to more places, to other displaced persons camps, so people could find us as well, just as we are looking for them. And then, we sat down and had a breakfast, which was lovely - as much as you wanted - plenty of bread, plenty of jam and cheeses, whatever you wanted. It was a normal restaurant you could say. That got us used to reasonable, normal behaviour and good food.

During the day, we just got together with others and talked and got to know other people, which was very, very good, finding out where they came from, where they had lived and everything about them. It was interesting to meet people. We didn't exactly know what was going to happen until the Jewish Brigade came to visit us. The purpose of it was for them to persuade us to be taken to Palestine. Most of us agreed, but we weren't quite sure if any of our family survived, so we weren't in a hurry to agree to go. Some people left straight away.

It was a nice place there with all the boys and girls, but we were separated into different blocks. We would be talking to girls and yes, we made friends with girls, and it became like normal dating, you know, although it was very short-lived. People met up with a girl and then met them the next day and the next day, until the transports split people up again. I don't remember how many there would have been in Salzburg in the first displaced persons camp, but the way they split us up was maybe twenty or so people in each open top wagon. What they did was that they covered everyone with sheets. I think the reason was to smuggle them through to Italy.

I remember that the four of us didn't go. We stayed behind, and what we did was we made our own way. We left when eventually we all realised we'd had enough in this camp. Most of the others had already gone with the Jewish Brigade because they had about six trucks to take them to Italy. So, we did it all on our own. As I said before, the Belgian and the Greek kids were older, so I think they had a bit more sense. We actually made our way to Italy by hitching lifts here and there, and on buses and trains. We ended up crossing the border, which was a nightmare.

Chapter 18

Checking one more List

Sam shuffled himself forward a few inches on the couch so that he was perched closer to the edge of the seat. He had a smile on his face as he did this; it's clear that he was recalling a story or a moment, and he was eager to tell it:

> Crossing the border from Salzburg to Innsburg took place a couple of days later over a mountain that was very, very high. As we got to the border, we could see there were guards with guns and turbans and they shouted, "Stop! Stop!" So, we stopped.
>
> I was a bit nervous. I didn't know who they were or what they wanted. They asked us, "Where are you going?" We told them we were survivors from the camps, we were supposed to make our way to Italy and that we were just trying to get through. But they asked us more and more questions, "Why were we going to Italy?" We said we were meeting up with the Jewish Brigade to go to Palestine. I remember one going into the office and the other one guarding us, and he must have asked someone some questions.
>
> I was looking at the other boys to see if they were worried, but they seemed okay. Anyway, the guard came out and he said it was okay, and that they had just let through some lorries with the Jewish

Brigade, and so he even pointed the way that they went. He said we could go free.

We hitched and hitched and took buses in Italy. Every time we went on a bus, or a train, to go from one place to another, when the guard came to ask us for tickets, we just said we were survivors from the camps, and they just left us alone. We were already clothed quite well and we had small bags with other clothes and some food. I remember the first place we got to in Italy was Modena Academi Militari.

When we got there, we met part of the Salzburg transport that had travelled a few days before, and we joined them, and from there on, we were part of the immigrants going to Palestine.

The Academi Militari was a big military building, and it was very comfortable. We slept in proper beds, and the food was reasonably good. They started to register us, taking note of all our details. Every time that the Jewish Brigade met us, they asked us lots of questions to gather information and see if they could try and put families back together.

So, we were there possibly up to ten days. Then, we went to Bologna. I don't know why they didn't take us straight to Bari where there was a port, but they took us to Bologna to another army camp, and we were there for several weeks. We were well looked after. We had enough food because the morning breakfast was plenty, and when we came back for lunch there was plenty more, and at night, there was also plenty. But we went out to look at the town, you know, and we came back at night to sleep. Eventually, we ended up in Bari where the ship would be arriving from Palestine.

A point I made to Sam was that during this whole period and the way he was describing it - after he had already described the years of hell, now he was describing this part of his adventure and it almost sounds like a bit of a holiday. Was that how it felt?

The feeling was fantastic, but what always came back to us, were thoughts about the family, and we became sad again. But otherwise, we were free, and everything was free for us.

We didn't have any money, but we didn't need any. People treated us really nicely, because when we said we were survivors from the camps, they helped us. I remember one time, we were sitting in a cafe and there you had to have money when you ordered a coffee or anything. When the waitress came over and we explained, in German, that we had just come out of the camps and we had no money yet, they just let us order without paying. You know, the situation was unbelievable. It just seemed like a dream, but a pleasant dream compared to the nightmares going back months before.

At this point in the story back then, Sam was sixteen years old. Apart from when he talked about his family, did he feel like a normal sixteen-year-old?

I still felt very damaged. I still did not feel complete because I wasn't with my family. But I felt a lot better percentage wise, I would say probably only fifty percent, because I was still missing the main thing in my life, which had left me about eighteen months before. I knew that I was not likely to see half of my family again. I knew that I would never see my mother, or my sister, although I did think that I might see my brother.

When we were in Bari, we were also in barracks, like army barracks. It was reasonably comfortable while we were waiting for the transport to Palestine. One day, a new transport truck came, and I met this boy. He came over and we started exchanging names and information about each other. I mentioned to him my name was Szmulek Gontarz, and he thought for a minute, and he said, "Szmulek Gontarz. Have you got a sister called Sala Gontarz?"

Sam started crying. He tried to speak but he couldn't. He looked at his hands and then looked away, down to his feet. He stared at the floor and cried. Robbie moved over from his chair and over to Sam. He perched himself on the arm of the chair and crouched down to place a kiss on his dad's head. He held him silently for a few seconds and then tried to talk him gently round.

Sam spluttered through his tears:

That part immediately kills me ... it kills me.

Robbie breathed deeply. This hurt him too. A tear rolled down Robbie's face, which he swiftly wiped away. He reassured Sam that we understood. He asked him if he wanted a drink.

Sam leant forward and helped himself to a drink. He put the glass down slowly and continued:

> I said to the boy, "Yes, how do you know?" He said he was just liberated from Belsen, which was like a displaced persons camp in Germany, and probably just like we were doing, they all mixed together, boys and girls and they just exchanged names. So I asked him questions and he told me he had been with Sala just a few days before. I couldn't believe it and to be honest, I didn't believe it. It was too crazy to think of.

> My three friends were there when this happened. They heard it all. So, immediately, they all said to me, "Szmulek, we are going to Germany to find her."

Chapter 19

From Hell to Heaven

Sam broke down and began sobbing again, and this time, Robbie decided it was best to just let him go through it. Robbie mouthed to me the words, "I've never heard him say it like this" and when I looked at Sam, I realised he was totally re-living one of the most poignant and emotional moments of his life, undoubtedly for the very first time since it happened. Sam was completely lost in his thoughts, feelings and emotions. He was consumed by memories. I imagined him stood there as a sixteen-year-old boy in that camp that day, talking to that random stranger who just told him that possibly, his sister was still alive.

He looked up at me and wiped away the tears from behind his glasses, and then he smiled a warm and beautiful smile:

> And so, the next morning that's what we did. We started to go all the way back to Germany, and they did it with me, my friends. We hitchhiked because we still didn't have any money yet.

> We had travelled so much in those recent weeks and I think that I must have been lost just thinking about whether I would see my sister again. I realised that she could have gone by the time we arrived at where she was supposed to be. She could have been moved on, and I might never be able to find her

again. So I was excited but I didn't want to have too much hope in my heart.

Finally, we got to Belsen and we got into the camp there. I started explaining to them who I was looking for. I told them my sister's name, Sala Gontarz, and luckily one of the women in the office remembered that there was a girl there by that name. She said, "Yes, we have a Sala Gontarz here."

I was immediately relieved that she was still there. I hadn't missed her, that was the main thing. But I didn't really get time to think because a few minutes later, she came in.

Sam broke down sobbing, before the words were even out of his mouth. This was the deepest sobbing that I had ever heard him make. His entire body shook as he cried. His head was down, his chin against his chest, and his hunched over shoulders rose and fell in staggered jerks as he cried.

Robbie and I looked at each other, not knowing what was best to do. I started to get out of my chair, but Robbie was up quicker and went over to embrace his dad. He wrapped his arms around him, and I thought to myself that Robbie wasn't hugging his ninety-year-old father in that moment; I thought he was clutching on to a little sixteen-year-old boy who had just been magically reunited with his sister following a separation of eighteen months, and after believing that she was already dead.

After a good few minutes of crying and sobbing, Sam slowly regained some composure and wiped his cheeks with the back of his hands. His eyes were red and swollen when he began to talk again:

I couldn't believe it. There she was. She was there in front of me. That was the best time since the liberation. She came into the hut with the woman from the camp and we just grabbed each other. She was dressed in civilian clothes, which must have been given to her.

When I first saw her, she didn't look the same because she was still very, very thin, but the face didn't fool me. I knew straight away that it was Sala. We started hugging each other. There were many tears and we couldn't talk. All we both said was, "Thank God, thank God, thank God."

Don't forget, it was eighteen months since I had seen her and I didn't believe that she had survived because I knew where she went to in Birkenau, on the other side, where they were sent to the gas chambers and the crematorium

We hugged each other for a long time. We didn't even speak. When we started asking questions, she asked me about Srulek, our brother, and I asked about my mother and so on. I remember we sat down and talked for ages.

She asked me about how me and my brother became separated. I told her what happened to me in Birkenau, that my brother was taken away from me, and I don't know what had happened to him since, or whether he was alive or not. She said she had been looking at the list, because they also had the list in Belsen, and she didn't even see my name, and so she believed it was possible that our brother was alive.

But she then said, "I have to tell you about our mother. I'm sorry to tell you she went to the crematorium. I know that. I saw it." She continued, "I managed to separate myself from marching as we felt that this march was not taking us to a nice place. Some of us managed to get away, not from the camp, but from this march."

I was just very, very pleased and very happy that Sala and I had found each other. At least I now had one member of my family. At least we had each other.

I think it was the Greek boy, who must have heard about a displaced persons camp in Germany near Munich called Feldafing, and that if we got ourselves there, we would be able to get Aliyah to Palestine, because that was what we all wanted.

I told her that I wanted her to come with me. I didn't ask her, I told her and she said, "Yes, but I've got a friend here and we are very close, so I've got to ask her." She didn't go in to get her friend. She asked one of the women in the office to get her friend for her, and she did. I think that Sala didn't want to let me out of her sight, nor me her.

Sala's friend came into the office and she agreed immediately to join us, so there were six of us now.

I think we went almost immediately, later that same afternoon, to start our travels to Feldafing, the six of us. We were free again, and I had a family. Finally, I had a family.

We sat in silence for a few minutes. Sam looked towards the picture of his sister that loomed down on him from across the room, on the sideboard. His lips formed a gentle smile, and I could tell that he wasn't in the room with me anymore, he was in that office being re-united with his sister all over again. Robbie smiled at me through the silence. We were both thinking the same thing - what were the chances of them finding each other in the way they did? I contemplated how life worked in very mysterious ways, taking everything from these two children, orphaning them through the horrors of the war camps, and yet somehow, bringing them back together in the end.

Sam looked back to me and started up again:

I don't think that if I had been on my own I would have been as knowledgeable and confident to go and do as the Greek boy did. He really was our leader and we trusted him. I did especially. It took more than one day to get to Feldafing. It was a long way because part of it, we had to do by train where we sat on top of the carriages. You might have seen that some of the survivors did this to travel from one place to another. That's how we did it, because we didn't have any money yet. It was pretty crazy.

Eventually, we ended up in Munich and from there, we managed to get to Feldafing; it was only a thirty-minute ride. We managed to get a proper train and we joined the main camp at Feldafing.

I asked Sam if he could tell me the story that his sister had told him about her journey through the camps?

Her journey was one of suffering. What she went through was very similar to me. The work she did was a different type, some sort of forced labour. She was in Birkenau more or less the same time as I was. She said that she did some work in parts of it, but when she went to Auschwitz, and it must have been the same time as I did, she would have gone with the women's transport.

If I would have known she was alive and in Auschwitz, I probably would have met up with her. But obviously I didn't know that she was there or where she was in the camp. Evidently though, she was in there at the same time as me.

When Auschwitz was liberated and they were taken to another camp like I was, she went through the same marches as I did, but the girls' marches. The places she went to were exactly the same. First Melk, then Gunskirchen, then to Mauthausen, then Wels and somehow, we didn't meet up, even in Wels which was an open camp.

Once we settled down, first we had to wait to get registered, because every displacement persons camp you went in, you had to go to an office, introduce yourself and provide your personal details. They were displaying these names more and more on boards for people to try and find each other, but it was funny that she wasn't on any board and I wasn't, because she was obviously looking for a Gontarz, me and my brother, and I was looking for her, but we weren't on any of the boards.

Anyway, once we got to Feldafing, we introduced ourselves and we got settled in to a barrack. It was simple and comfortable. It wasn't luxurious but it was clean, with bunks of three high, women separate; men separate, but at least I knew I was with my sister in the next block, so we were quite happy. Then we started to talk because we were there for a while in Feldafing.

We didn't really do much. We were well looked after; the food was good. We got up as early as possible. We had a big assembly room where we went for breakfast. We had a decent lunch, proper soup and proper boiled potatoes and meat, chicken, you know, like in a restaurant.

There was a committee which looked after this particular displaced persons camp and there, you could go in and have a chat with them, and explain yourself, describe exactly what had happened to you and they put it all on record.

Sam broke off briefly and paused.

You know, Robbie, when we found out about my past from the internet, I think it was from the information I gave in Feldafing. I disclosed a lot about myself there. I remember it took a long time for me to sit and explain. But anyway, eventually, I told them everything that I could remember. And then, I never really spoke of it again properly, until now.

We weren't in locked camps anymore. We could move around. I could see Sala whenever I wanted and she could see me. We went walking about and talking and exchanging conversation about home. We were still missing one name, Srulek, you know. We still didn't know if he was alive or not. We gave his name, and I explained exactly what happened in Birkenau and how we were separated and they put it all down on paper.

Then, General Eisenhower came to visit and this was rather a nice experience. He came and looked at our barracks. He called a meeting to speak to all the survivors. It was traumatic because when he came in, all the survivors gathered around him. We knew who he was. He was in his American uniform and he had all his bodyguards. He asked us if we were comfortable and the answers came back to him that yes, we were, although of course, it was not really like home.

He spoke in English so everything he said had to go through an interpreter into our Yiddish. Eventually, he said, "Come with me" and we all followed him. He walked past nice apartment blocks and shouted for the German people inside to get out. Then, you saw the Germans running, literally running and Eisenhower said that whoever wanted to use these homes, they could take them.

The four of us ended up in a lovely place called Villa Park. I've got photographs which I will get out to show you. Honestly, it was a beautiful place, probably worth millions, millions. We found out that during the war, the Hitler Youth occupied that villa. So, the four of us took it. But it was all really down to the Greek boy. He was brave and very confident. But Villa Park was reasonably empty when we went in. We could see there were many rooms, so we picked the ones we wanted. It had a huge, big balcony overlooking Starnberger See. It was like going from hell to heaven. We had clean sheets and there was a kitchen, and the Belgian boy, who must have known how to cook, became busy straight away cooking and organising everything. He went to the main restaurant, and he organised all sorts of food, so he could do the cooking for us. We had plenty of food and we had a really great time when we were there.

Again, I don't really know how long we were there as remembering time becomes very weird with me. I can't place time, but I will tell you it was not days or weeks; we were there for probably a few months.

My sister was in a different block with the girls. They didn't mix in the same blocks, you know, but we knew where they were, and we saw each other during the day and we would eat together. We enjoyed life again. We did what we called organising which meant we took stuff from the Germans and from the farms. We took whatever we could.

We saw each other every day, several times a day actually and this went on for a while. Although we were free, we didn't do much apart from swim, have fun and eat.

I asked Sam if he could remember the feelings of being a sixteen-year-old boy and now having the freedom of Villa Park, wandering around it and discovering all the rooms, after being in the ghetto and the camps since he was eleven.

It was a very mixed feeling to be honest. I was happy in the first place but then we always ended up sad because we weren't with our family. As happy as we were about having freedom and meals, we missed our family terribly. And that was how it was.

Robbie had left a small pile of photographs on the table between Sam and I. I picked a few of them up and played with them in my hands whilst Sam talked. I noticed one of Sam with the three other boys standing on a jetty that looked out onto a vast, beautiful lake. I asked Sam about this.

Yeah, that was the four of us. We actually went swimming from that jetty. That jetty is sometimes called Starnberger See but it is still in Feldafing, so we went there quite often. It was a walk from our house to the lake, several miles, but sometimes we would walk it. It was an absolutely beautiful lake, and we went swimming there. The four of us always went everywhere together which was probably a good thing for all of us.

Before the war, I learnt swimming in a pond, a dirty pond, as we didn't have pools in Poland, so I already knew a bit about how to swim, but I wasn't a swimmer yet. I really learned to swim in Feldafing. But I wasn't a strong swimmer. I could just about hold myself on the water, the same as the older boys. Genek, unfortunately, wasn't a good swimmer and he tried it one time and he nearly drowned, so the other boys shlepped him out and, you know, helped him to get back to shore. And he was very lucky because he could have died and after that, he never went swimming again.

We used to go there a lot. We would walk around the lake, smoking cigarettes and throwing stones into the water. We would throw stones into the air and see who could get them up the highest. Then we would race along the jetty and see who could be the first one in the water.

I was struck by the stark contrast of this image of incredible tranquillity and beauty with the harsh, ugly, evil of the concentration camps. I asked Sam how he was able to marry the two extremes that had taken place in his life over such a short period of time.

As happy as we were on one side to be free and do what we wanted when we wanted to, there was still a sadness within us and that lasted a long time. At least I had my sister with me, thank God.

Robbie asked his dad about the mischief they got up to. He clearly knew that there were stories to tell. Sam laughed in anticipation:

Feldafing was about thirty minutes from Munich, so the nearest place to go shopping or to look around in the city was Munich. But we became pretty wild, especially the Greek boy. When he went on a train, and he saw Germans sitting somewhere, he kicked them out. And because we were survivors of the camps, the Germans already sensed who we were and that we were in the displaced persons camp, so they immediately left.

At the end of the day, we had not been brought up properly. We had been in ghettos and in concentration camps and so we didn't know what was right or wrong or how to behave. I think the Germans were actually scared, especially the women, because if we went into a compartment and we wanted to sit down, we asked them to go, and then they left before the train started. We were the bosses for a while at least. We would take their suitcases and If we went through a tunnel, we would throw the suitcases out the window and then go back for them afterwards. There were all kinds of things like this that went on. I can't remember exactly as there were so many. We didn't know any different.

Eventually, the American army who were the occupiers at the time stopped us doing this. If we wanted to go to Munich, they arranged for us to go by their transport. The transport consisted of big lorries and the survivors were banned now from all public transport. It wasn't just us, there were lots of groups of young kids running wild, running absolutely wild, doing whatever they wanted.

I look back on this period of my life and it was a good time although it was not a normal time. But it was something that we seemed to enjoy after what we had been through. From that hell became this heaven. We had enough food, we had enough clothes, we had comfortable accommodation. We were free in lovely surroundings, because Feldafing was a beautiful place, a holiday place actually, and everything was alright except what was missing, part of the family. I was happy, at least for now.

Chapter 20

A Dog's Life

As Sam finished speaking about Feldafing and Villa Park, Robbie disappeared into the next room and emerged moments later with another pile of old, black and white photographs. He sifted through a few of them in his hand and then passed them to me. One of the photos showed two young men sitting on a balcony, one is in swimming shorts and the other in a shirt and trousers. The smarter dressed boy is stroking a dog. Robbie suggested to Sam that he tell me about his dog

Sam looked over at me, and saw I had the photograph of the boys with the dog. He chuckled:

Oh, yes. I must tell you. A dog attached itself to me, you know, on one of my walks. Dogs always do that to me actually - more than people. He was a beautiful dog. As I was walking, I think I was taking my laundry to a woman to do the washing for me, and this dog attached itself to me and followed me all the way back to the villa. We named him, well I named him, Waldmann, which is German for forest man.

He was a dog with brown and white patches. I'm not sure what breed; he was a bit of everything. I started liking him and then, in the end, I started loving him. He went back with me to Villa Park, and he stayed with me all the time, and I thought he'd go after a bit but he didn't. He stayed there and I got used to him and he followed me everywhere. He looked up to me like, you know, like I'd known him for years. I've got other pictures of me with him on the balcony at Villa Park. On the picture, you can see the way he looks at me. So, obviously, we looked after him. We fed him, the other boys liked him as well. But he was really my dog.

On one occasion, me and the boys decided to go down to Starnberger See, which is only a few miles from Feldafing, but we were going by train and so the dog followed us all the way to the train station. We went on the train and that was that. I thought the dog would go back as normal and he would be waiting on the grounds of the Villa when I got back. But, unbeknown to us, when we got to Starnberger and we were at the place where you hire the boats, all of a sudden, we turned around and the dog came running to us - you've never seen anything like it. It was like a dream. He had followed us all the way there. The train doesn't go that fast, but I mean it's a train, so you know, it goes faster and faster, but that crazy dog followed us all the way. So of course, we got him into the boat, and we went about our business as normal with him there, but it was absolutely comical really.

So, for a while, I had a dog, and it was a lovely experience for me. He followed me wherever I went. I went to the restaurants in the morning to have breakfast and he followed me. I would sit on the balcony sunbathing and he would be there on my knee. It was really good.

Chapter 21

One Scruffy Terrier

Some months later, when I had listened back to Sam telling me about the dog who had adopted him, I asked Robbie if they had had any pets when he was growing up. He told me a few stories about the dogs they had:

> Shortly after they got married, my mum and dad got a Bedlington Terrier and the dog's name was Wriggles. He was a boy dog. Now, according to everyone, this was the most fantastic dog. I don't really remember it that well, because I was very young.
>
> But one thing that I do know is that the dog used to sleep at the bottom of their bed, and so, if my dad came in late at night, which he often did, when he tried to get into bed, the dog would attack him because the dog loved my mum so much, he was protective of her. My dad hated that dog.
>
> But anyway, that dog passed away, unfortunately, and then my mum got another dog, a miniature Schnauzer called Shar, and he was like family, but my mum was still very upset about Wriggles, the Bedlington Terrier.

She was standing in her bedroom one day and she looked out the window and at the top of the driveway, she saw this scruffy dog just standing there, and my mother swears blind it was a year to the day that she'd lost Wriggles.

Anyway, she went downstairs, called my dad, they opened the front door, and this scruffy little dog came running up to them. Now this dog, when it arrived at the door, was absolutely filthy, it had newspaper matted into it and it was in a horrible state.

I came home from school, and in the back yard I could see this scruffy, smelly thing, so bad that you didn't even really want to touch it, but my mum told me and my dad to take it to the vets and get it checked out.

We took it there and the vet wouldn't see to it until it got bathed, so me and my dad took the dog to a poodle parlour nearby and left the dog with them for an hour or so.

We came back an hour or so later, and we were sitting there waiting and they brought this dog out, and I just looked at the dog and thought, 'Ah, that's a nice dog.' The woman said to me, "Don't you want your dog?"

I couldn't believe it. You have never in your life seen a dog so beautiful. And even the dog was proud. You could see it in the way she walked and she had this little hair do. So, we came out the shop and my mum was sitting there in the car waiting for us. As soon as I came out the door, my mum said to me straight away, "I knew that dog was a Bedlington Terrier."

We took her straight back to the vets, and the vet inspected her. He could tell that she'd been tied up with string around the neck because it had burned all the fur off there and she had a scar.

Anyway, the vet immediately wrote out these papers that said that we legally owned the dog because it had been neglected.

She became a real member of the family, but for some reason, she became my dog, even though the dog was loved by everyone. She ended up being my dog because she slept in my bedroom on my bed.

After a period of time though, she started developing epileptic fits. Now, when she first started, it wasn't too bad. She'd have a little five minute one where she was shaking, and then when she came out of it, she was just like a normal dog again.

But as these things went on, they seemed to last longer and became more severe. We got to the stage where we knew we had a problem. I came home late one night, and I went into my bedroom and the dog was on my beanbag having a terrible fit. I sat with it for about half an hour and then I had to take her to the emergency vets. They kept her overnight, and then the next morning, the vet said to us, "She's recovered from the fit, but you've got a big decision to make as a family, because she's gone blind."

I was absolutely heartbroken but as a family, we felt the best decision was to have her put to sleep because it just wouldn't have been fair to her with the epilepsy and the blindness, but it broke all of our hearts.

Chapter 22

Day Trip to Munich

Sam continued his story about the time he and his sister Sala were staying in Feldafing:

> My sister was quite comfortable where she lived and she made lots of friends, girlfriends, in the block where she lived, and we introduced each other to our friends, so we became like one big family.
>
> I don't know what they were planning to do, but they decided to go to Munich. Now at that particular time, we weren't allowed to go by train, just for a short while, because of the behaviour from us towards the German people. So, the transport was actually organised by the Americans, you know. They provided transport for whoever wanted to go to Munich. It was only about twenty odd kilometres, so whoever wanted to go there just booked in the morning with somebody in the station, and then later, you were picked up and you went.
>
> This particular time, my sister and four of her friends decided to go. I don't know whether it was just a day out in Munich, whether they were going to buy something, I don't know. Anyway, that day I had a bad cold, a chesty cold, so I went to hospital in an ambulance. It wasn't that serious, but Feldafing was a big, displaced persons camp, so they took me to hospital.

I think that I probably wouldn't have taken myself to hospital, but we had people who looked after us. They came to the Villa to see how we were and I must have reported that I didn't feel well and I think that is why I went.

I remember Sala came in the morning to see me, and she asked me if it was alright if she went, because she always asked. Although she was older than me, she always asked me if it was alright if she did something.

While I was in the hospital, a bit later, getting towards early afternoon, my friends came to the hospital and I could see by their faces that they had something to tell me that was not pleasant. As they started talking, I said, "What happened to Sala?"

They told me that the truck that she had been travelling to Munich in had been hit by a military vehicle and overturned onto a railway and all the girls had been killed instantly, including Sala.

I was devastated. I couldn't believe it. I said, "Are you sure she died?" They said yes. There were seven girls that died, four of them were Sala and three of her best friends, and three other girls that they didn't know.

I was absolutely, totally devastated. Obviously, I started crying and asking lots of questions, but I mean, I couldn't think properly. I told the boys to just get me out of there and take me to the place where, if anybody died they took them, where they got them ready for burial and to do prayers and say Kaddish - so my friends helped me to get to this place.

I was devastated for days and weeks and weeks. I had lost her all over again.

Sam broke down and sobbed, violently. His entire body shook as the emotion coursed through his tiny body. The sound of him crying was possibly one of the saddest I have ever heard in my life.

I was totally stunned by what Sam had just revealed. I was not expecting it, at all. I was certain that life was now going to be kind to him, and he would now go on to build a life with his sister.

It sounds cliched, but I literally had my mouth wide-open, aghast at this latest twist in Sam's life. Robbie looked at me and shook his head. He knew what was coming but it had still shocked him. I just couldn't believe it.

Some minutes later, Sam managed to gather himself. He wiped away tears with the back of his hand, and slowly spoke:

Now, at the cemetery in Feldafing, all their stones have been put together. I can show you the picture because I have been back to visit her since.

I wanted to confirm if Sam had actually attended a funeral for Sala.

Yes. I attended a funeral. I think it was a few days after, for some reason or other. Maybe, they wanted to find out how, and why, and what - I don't know. I know normally, Jewish burials are straight away but that was a different situation there.

I vaguely remember the funeral, though. It was a blur. It was the only funeral of my family members that I attended, because as you know, I wasn't there to attend for the others. Well, obviously, it was just very, very emotional for me crying, sobbing and trying to get over it like normal people do after a family death.

But this was more than just a normal person because she was a survivor, and after eighteen months apart, we were back together again. We were living again. We took the time to plan a future together, and then this happened.

Sam started to cry again. The room felt tense, perhaps more so than at any other time in the interviews. After a minute or so of sobbing, Sam leaned forward and reached for a drink. Robbie broke the tension further by asking his dad about his pals, Genek and the two other boys.

Sam slowly put his drink down and settled back into position on the couch:

They were always with me, right to the end when I left. From Feldafing to me coming to England, they looked after me. They're the ones who came into the hospital to tell me the news.

That was the saddest part. I had lost the rest of my family, that was hard enough, but that was the saddest part of anything, because she had survived.

Tears continued to roll down Sam's cheeks. He didn't stop to sob, he just let the tears roll down, and he carried on talking:

I was so angry at God, at the universe, at everything. In fact, from what I remember, I think I felt a bit guilty as well. I don't know why, maybe because I was in hospital, maybe because I wasn't with her, but I felt a bit guilty. I think I feel guilty even now about it. I always felt that if I hadn't gone and brought her from Bergen-Belsen, possibly, she could have survived and gone to Israel. But, at the same time, nothing in this world can replace the months we spent together after the war. As I said, we saw each other every day. She lived in a different villa, but she either came to see us or I went to see her.

I asked Sam if he had any specific memories of that time.

Well, I was very subdued for some time, several weeks, but life goes on, and though you don't get over it, you get used to it and learn to live with the way things are. It's really only when we discussed it like we are doing now, you know, then it all comes back, and the emotion comes back and it hurts.

I remember Sala and I had conversations after the war about our initial home life, you know, what we used to do and how we lived, and because we were a poor family, we weren't a wealthy family, but we kids had a good life. You know, how our parents did everything for us they could, and it didn't always mean money, but we still had a lot of affection, and we discussed that a lot.

We also discussed my brother Srulek, because at the time, I didn't know that my brother was shot on a death march walking from one camp to another. We didn't find out until I came to England and by chance, I met somebody who was with him on that particular march, and they actually witnessed him being shot.

So we discussed the good times - where we lived and everything else, and we planned a lot. And the main plan was to go to Palestine.

I wondered what happened in the next few weeks after Sala died.

Well, I was with the boys, and we were very, very close - Genek and the others. And, of course, I was depressed. I was subdued but I still wanted to go to Palestine. Palestine was always our dream.

One day, I received a letter which came to the office within the camp. People were looking for me, my relatives from England. They brought me a letter, and it said that my relatives wanted me to come over to England. They found out that I was alive.

I went back to the office in Feldafing, and I explained to them the situation, and they already had papers prepared for me to travel to France by train. They arranged everything, and from France, I was to go to England. They asked me if I wanted to go and I said that with them being relatives, of course I wanted to. So that was the third time a plan to go to Palestine was abandoned.

They made preparations for me and they prepared a date, and all the boys went with me to the train to see me off. We hugged and we kissed, and we waved until we couldn't see each other anymore. And that was it, that was the end of Feldafing. That was the last time I was ever with the boys.

Chapter 23

Tea with Milk

We were now going to hear about a new chapter in Sam's story as he made his way to England and his relatives.

> I don't remember sitting on the train for too long because it picked me up at the station and it was a short enough journey to Munich. But I was very sad. The way I felt was mixed because first of all, I was leaving the boys and not going to Palestine, and I had tears in my eyes, but then on the other hand, I thought well, at least I'm going to my family. So, it was really mixed feelings.

> Then I had to get on to a different train, which took me over the border to France. When I got to France, they already had papers for where I was going, to a hotel to stay for a few days. I stayed in France for about four or five days, just under a week.

> I remember I was allocated into a hotel in Paris which was quite comfortable, maybe not like the Ritz but a nice hotel. And I was getting fat already. I had clothes which weren't anything special, but they weren't concentration camp striped clothes anymore, and I went out and I took walks.

> I couldn't speak to anyone because they were all speaking French or English and I didn't speak either of those languages. So, I just went out and walked

about and then I would get back in the evening, and they always informed me at the desk if there was any post for me. Whenever I got a call, they had to have an interpreter in the hotel to tell me what the message was all about. Then they got me ready again to go on a train, and then the boat took me right over to England, Calais to Dover. I had a bag, not a suitcase, with a couple of shirts, some underpants, not a lot of stuff, the bare minimum.

When I got there, my cousin, who was called Easy, was already waiting for me. He recognised me. I don't know how. He must have seen photographs from my family before the war. He came over to me. "Szmulek, Szmulek," he said, so I knew immediately that this was the person who was meeting me.

There was a coffee shop almost right when you got off the boat. We went there. He got me a drink, a cup of tea and he asked for milk, and I thought it was strange - tea with milk. We never had it with milk at home; we had tea with lemon and sugar. So, I said, "Oh, is that tea?" I thought maybe it's coffee or something. He said, "Yeah, yeah, you'll enjoy it."

We spoke in Yiddish. He wasn't speaking fluently like I was but we could converse. We could understand each other and I started asking questions about where we were going and how long it would take us. He said we were waiting for the train, and we were going to Manchester, and it would take about three hours. Then we were going to a house, and I would meet my auntie and my other cousins and that was it.

We talked on the train quite a bit. He kept asking me about the camps, and I answered. I don't remember volunteering much at that time, but I just answered questions that he asked me as well as I could.

I asked Sam if, on his trip from Feldafing, he looked out the window on the train at the changing landscapes moving him from Germany to Manchester.

Well to me, England didn't look as nice as when I was traveling through Germany. The landscape and everything, all the lakes that you passed in Germany were in fact, much better. But I took it all in as it passed by. And when we got off the train at Piccadilly station, we got a taxi because he didn't have a car, and we went to his house.

So, timewise, it was now early evening. When we got out of the taxi and into the house, my auntie got up and grabbed hold of me and cried. She was just happy to see that one of the family members from Europe was still alive. There were thirteen cousins altogether originally, but only some survived. The ones in Manchester didn't all live in that house. There was Easy and two girls, but then the next day, people started coming from other houses, and most of the children who lived nearby came to meet me, to see me and for me to get introduced to them.

Did Sam have a room of his own in his new home?

Yes. This house was a big house, three stories high, with a basement. And as you walked in into a passageway, straight ahead was the lounge with the kitchen on the left-hand side. I came into the lounge and all of my cousins sat down and my aunt started asking me questions. I was very tired. I really wanted to go to bed. It wasn't night-time yet, but it was early evening. So, I had another cup of tea there and they made me something to eat, and then I got to bed.

The following day, it just carried on like normal, and I just simply got used to it, to this house. They treated me reasonably well. But there were signs very quickly that I wouldn't be very happy there for long, maybe because I had been incarcerated for so long that I just couldn't get used to being with my family again in one house.

I remember that after a few days, I asked my auntie if it was alright if I went out for a walk. She called Easy and she told him to write down the address of where we lived, so that if I got lost, I'd have to find a policeman, and the policeman would direct me where to go. So, I put the piece of paper in my pocket. Anyway, after I passed about three or four houses, I saw a bike on the left hand-side, leaning on the wall, so I grabbed the bike. I had never been on a bike, didn't know how to ride or anything. Anyway, I got on and I remember wobbling, but I just drove a few yards and all of a sudden, I heard a shout from behind me. I turned around. It was Easy. He was shouting, "Szmulek, Szmulek. Come back, come back."

I didn't know what he wanted. I didn't think I had done anything wrong at the time. So, I went back and I said, "What's up? What's the matter?" He said, "You can't just do that, take somebody's bike." "Well," I said. "But it was outside on the wall, it wasn't anybody's."

He explained to me and lectured me in Yiddish, and then the owner of the bike came out and they started talking in English, but I sort of understood what they meant. Easy told me all I needed to do was just say sorry. That was one of the first English words I learned, sorry.

This fellow, whose bike it was, turned out to be a very nice fellow actually, and he said to Easy to tell me that I could use the bike whenever I wanted, as long as I brought it back and put it in the same place.

The crazy thing was that I didn't realise that I had done anything wrong. Why did somebody keep a bike outside? It was in the morning, probably about between ten and eleven, you know, and I thought it was just there to use. I understood then that I had not been socialised. I didn't feel any guilt really, even afterwards. I was thinking, 'What did I do wrong?' But I realised that maybe I should have gone and asked or something, or just not bothered at all because I only wanted to go for a walk, so it wouldn't have mattered. Anyway, I didn't get lost. I didn't need to call the contact number.

But you see, the moral of this story was that even though, nearly two years after the liberation, I still wasn't normal. It wasn't a thing that a normal person would do, unless he was a thief, but I wasn't a thief. I did it just not realising that this was a wrong thing to do. These were the daily challenges I found adjusting to life after the camps.

Sam smiled at me. His story had come to a natural end at this point. This had been the longest session of any of the ones we had. The story was so gripping, and Sam had gone through so much in the process that it seemed the kindest thing to do was to get it over with in one session, and not make him go through it again.

It was a relatively high point to finish the session with and I commented on that. Sam shrugged.

As I broke the equipment down and packed up, Sam sat silently, eventually picking up his iPad and swiping away at various icons on the screen. Robbie and I talked, mainly about the disbelief at how the story had taken so many unbelievable turns, and the cruelty of him losing his sister after finding her again.

I bent down to give Sam a hug. As I was leaving, he shouted after me, "Send my love to the family?"

Robbie helped me carry the equipment out and pack it in the car. There wasn't much left to say, but we discussed arranging an evening meal with both our families. This was something we had talked about on several occasions. Sam was really keen to get both of our families together, and although we were too, our busy lifestyles hadn't yet made it possible.

We made a more solid promise to make it happen this time.

Chapter 24

Good Driver; Bad Driver

As part of his life in England, Sam had to learn to drive in order to transport his family to where they needed to go.

Unfortunately, driving skills were not his best.

Robbie once told me a story about how bad a driver his dad was, but also how his mother was a wonderful driver.

Sheila always drove manual cars, and where possible, she would choose sporty versions of the car, and she would drop gears and accelerate, and she just loved to drive.

Sam only ever drove automatic cars; he just felt they were more comfortable, and most importantly, safer. Tiny as he was, he would often barely be able to see over the steering wheel and he would grip on to that steering wheel like he was holding on for dear life.

And, when they would go out as a family, everyone would be trying to relax in the car, Sheila would be in the passenger seat and the kids would be in the back, and this was a time before seatbelts were a standard thing. But Sam had this weird technique whereby he would accelerate hard for a second and then immediately take his foot off the accelerator. So, they would all jerk and shudder all the way down the road like this, and he just couldn't help himself.

On one occasion, the family went over to America on holiday and were in Fort Lauderdale.

Sam had arranged to meet a couple of his friends out there. But, on this particular day, they were travelling around Florida, and Sam had hired this long, blue estate car, with wood panelling down the side of it. Sam had decided he was driving but straight away someone rammed into the back of him. It wasn't Sam's fault especially but as a tourist in a new city and driving a car far too big for him, he probably wasn't faultless either. So, the police came along and looked at the damage and thankfully there wasn't anything major, so they got back on the road again.

Sheila was becoming impatient with Sam's driving and so sitting in the passenger seat, she would give Sam instructions and it was clear that he was starting to feel the pressure. Accidentally, he took a wrong turn and steered them into the middle of a private airfield with an aeroplane coming into land. Sheila and the kids were screaming and shouting at him and he was panicking and didn't know what to do, but just in the nick of time, he managed to get the car into reverse and steer them to safety.

Sheila drove for the rest of the holiday.

Chapter 25

Feeling Complete, at Last

It became increasingly difficult for me to stop thinking about Sam's story in between my meetings with him. We had been getting together for almost six months now, on and off, and it had been an intense journey for all of us. Sam had finally shared the entirety of his story in the ghetto and concentration camps, and though there was still all the years from him arriving in England up to the present day to share, the hardest and most challenging stories had been told.

I had experienced my own family loss in those six months too, and as summer approached, I felt ready for a holiday, so we made plans for a couple of trips abroad, as soon as the kids finished school.

Robbie and I spoke regularly during the entire time of recording Sam's story. We chatted several times each week, often about his dad, but also just generally about our lives. We developed a great friendship and got to know each other well. Robbie often told me how much his dad felt comfortable and secure in telling me his story, and that was the greatest compliment I could hope to hear.

With Robbie living in the Lake District, it hadn't yet been feasible to get our families together. Our kids were similar in age, and from our conversations, it was clear that our wives would get on well. It just hadn't happened yet.

I also hadn't yet met Adrian, Robbie's older brother, and although I had heard loads about him throughout the year, our paths just hadn't crossed.

So, although we couldn't get all the clan together, Robbie and I arranged to meet Sam and Adrian for dinner one night in a local Italian restaurant.

I arrived at the restaurant first. I am always early to everything and spend a lot of time waiting around for other people. It had been a few weeks since I had last seen Sam and so when, eventually, he arrived at the restaurant, he looked a little more fragile than when I had last seen him.

He spotted me across the room, his eyesight had clearly not diminished in any way, and he waved over and smiled at me. He took a slow walk across the room, and it seemed like he knew everybody in the restaurant. People called his name, and he wandered over to chat to them, shaking hands and chatting away happily. He must have visited four tables before he finally arrived with me.

"Sorry Ricky, there's a few people here that I know," Sam said as he shook my hand.

"You know everybody, don't you?" I replied, helping Sam to take his coat off.

Robbie arrived, after parking the car. "Adrian can't make it unfortunately," he said as he pulled me in for a hug and then helped ease his dad into a chair, "Hopefully, next time, he'll make it."

The meal was lovely. It was great to spend time with Sam without the heaviness of him having to divulge his story. We talked about normal, everyday life: Family, friends, golf and football. Several times during the meal, people came over to the table who knew Sam, and I could see from their faces just how much they loved him. He had a unique charm and magic, and a cheeky, mischievous glint in his eye. He had the lines, or the schtick as he would call it, to disarm anybody and make them laugh. For his tiny frame, he had the personality and charisma of a giant, and cliched as it may sound - he truly lit up the room. It felt like he was a celebrity presence in the restaurant.

At some point in the meal, the conversation came up about a possible trip to Poland and to visit Auschwitz. Although Sam had been back there once before, when he was in his sixties, he had never been there with Robbie and Adrian, and he expressed that it was unfinished business for him until he did. Sam asked if I would accompany them on the trip, and I was deeply honoured to be included in what would undoubtedly be a poignant and powerful trip.

The trip he planned would be to go back and find the apartments of his childhood, the area he lived while in the ghetto, and to visit Birkenau, Auschwitz and possibly Mauthausen. I sensed Robbie was conflicted. We spoke about it later. He wanted to do this important pilgrimage, but he was worried how it could affect Sam, ninety-years-old at that time, and becoming ever more fragile. The trip would be intense physically and emotionally; it would also be further complicated by having to arrange dialysis treatment at a hospital for Sam every couple of days. Sam was determined though, and history had already proved that there was no stopping him when he made his mind up.

As it turned out, the dates that Robbie and Sam eventually organised for the trip fell on the exact same dates that I had booked a family holiday in Italy. So, they made the necessary arrangements to return to Poland, just the three of them, and set off on a pilgrimage to find the places of Sam's childhood.

I was truly flattered to have been included in Sam's plans to take his boys back to Poland, but I also had a deeper sense that this was to be a poignant trip for the three of them, and I didn't want to get in their way.

Also, if I had accompanied them, I would have been tempted to film and document the trip, which would have meant that Sam and the boys would have been more self-conscious with the camera and microphone around, and I would miss out on the reality of the experience by watching it through a viewfinder.

The decision was taken away from me anyhow when our dates clashed. So, as I set off for Italy with my family, after a challenging first half to our year and with the aim of the trip being to recharge and relax. Sam, Robbie, and Adrian made their way to Poland with the intention of revisiting some of the greatest tragedies of their family's history.

I thought about them on the day we travelled to Italy, knowing that they were embarking on their journey too. I imagined Sam being wheeled through the airport like a king on his mobile throne, and knowing that he would be charming everybody he met with his cheeky smile and his charismatic charm. But, I also knew the trip would be harrowing for him, and I have to admit I was worried how it might affect him.

Robbie messaged me a few times during their trip, and sent me a couple of pictures, but they were just pictures of the three of them smiling in ordinary locations. He didn't send me any pictures of them in the camps or go into any detail about the trip, he just kept it light and said they were having a good trip.

When we both arrived back in England, Robbie was keen for us all to get together so that they could share the details of their trip. He didn't give much away, but the night after I returned from Italy I met Sam, Robbie and Adrian at a local Turkish restaurant, and prepared myself to hear their stories.

I arrived at the restaurant early, and I assumed I would be the first there and would be waiting around for a while as usual, but, as I walked in, a guy who was waiting in the waiting area of the restaurant got up and approached me, "Rik?"

"Adrian?" I replied, assuming that was who he must be. He smiled a huge, wide smile and it was immediately clear it was Adrian. Instinctively, we hugged and somehow, it didn't feel like the first time we had ever met. We were shown to our table, and we chatted like old friends while we waited for Sam and Robbie to arrive.

Our conversation flowed naturally. We both had heard a lot about each other over the last few months, and even before we met, we had felt like we knew one another.

"Dad loves you, Rik. He says he's never been able to open up about his past to anyone like he has been able to do with you," Adrian said at one point in the conversation.

There's very few compliments that I can take with any grace and without feeling awkward, but this compliment which I had heard from both Robbie and Adrian now, it felt truly special and an honour to receive.

We chatted briefly about the trip, but I could tell Adrian didn't want to give too much away without the others there.

Sam appeared in the doorway of the restaurant, Robbie had dropped him off and then gone on to park the car. Sam was wrestling with an umbrella after a typically Mancunian mid-summer downpour, and the restaurant manager helped him to fold the brolly and then showed him to our table. I was quite surprised when I saw him; he looked ten years younger than when I had last seen him. I told him too.

"Ricky, I have to tell you, I feel good; I feel younger," Sam replied as he shuffled along the bench next to Adrian and settled himself down.

We got talking and Sam told me that the trip had been amazing for him. He said it was the completion of a cycle. For him, going back to the place of his birth, and where he had lost most of his family in the ghetto and death camps, but this time with his two sons, themselves now grown men with families, was the greatest experience of his life.

Robbie arrived and sat down. He had an envelope in his hand, and he handed it to me. "Open it," he demanded.

I opened up the envelope and pulled out a pile of old black and white photographs. There were pictures of Sam as a baby with his whole family; Sam as a young boy; pictures of his mum, his dad, his sister and his brother; there were some pictures of Sam in Feldafing with Genek and the boys; pictures in Villa Park with Waldmann the dog. It was a bundle of incredible memories.

"Do what you need with them for the book Ricky," he told me.

Although I had never mentioned the possibility of actually writing Sam's book, my initial promise was to just record his story, I had become so entwined with Sam's story and with Robbie, and now also Adrian, that it had become an unspoken understanding that I would now try to help to get the story written and shared. Initially, I had been scared of the responsibility of taking on the project of telling Sam's story and potentially not being able to deliver on my promises, but now I had become a part of the story myself, and I was more fearful of the story not ever being told properly.

But even holding all these pictures felt like a heavy responsibility. These were all that Sam had left of his family; imagine if after all this time I was the one that lost them.

For the next hour or so, I listened intently as Sam told me the story of his return to Poland with his two sons. It was a gruelling trip even for the boys, but Sam, at ninety-years-old had managed it without a problem. He had dialysis on just one occasion during the trip, which is a break from his normal twice-weekly treatment when he was at home. And although the trip had been very emotional for him, and he had a few moments where he had broken down, he had found it exhilarating to return there with his boys.

Robbie told me how the worst moment for Sam had been when they arrived at Radegast station, the place where Sam and his family had experienced such a traumatic time when boarding the train that would take them to the camps after the Nazis had liquidated the Lodz ghetto. The memories of these terrible moments, and all the chaos and noise of that time, had overwhelmed Sam and he had needed ten minutes of solitude to sit in his wheelchair and cry it out.

But besides one or two other moments like this, Sam had found his return to Poland to be a cleansing process. Sam explained how kind everybody had been, not at all how he had last remembered the Polish people.

They had literally stumbled across the apartment Sam and his family had lived in before the war. Incredibly, it was the last remaining building on the street that hadn't been redeveloped yet. It was about to be knocked down, scaffolding was set up ready, but nevertheless, when Sam stood before it, it looked just like it had when he had last stood there in 1939. It was a graceful moment of serendipity and timing; a month later and the building would have been gone.

The builders saw Sam looking at the building from his wheelchair and came over to see him. He chatted to them and told them his story. They broke their safety protocol to allow him and the boys through the fencing and into the courtyard. Sam stood there with tears in his eyes, trying to find the window where his mum had stood and thrown down his sandwiches to him.

One evening, Sam and the boys were hungry and wandered into a part of town that in 1939 Jews weren't even allowed into. Nowadays, it is a beautiful, modern courtyard with shops, bars and restaurants, many of them serving Jewish dishes. Sam sat there eating his 'Haimishe' food, as he called it, and looking out over an area once forbidden to him, his two boys by his side. They raised a glass to each other, a 'L'Chaim', and Sam described how at that moment, he felt complete, for the first time in his life. Robbie took a picture of his dad sat there in the square, beaming from ear to ear.

Later that night, when I got home, I scanned every single one of the photographs on my home printer, just so I could return the originals to Robbie. I was taking no chances.

Chapter 26

Storytelling Quandary

I spent the next month or so transcribing Sam's interviews, with any spare time that I had, which is easier said than done with two young kids, a crazy dog, and running two businesses. Nevertheless, I dedicated as many late night and weekend hours as I could.

It was a slow and painstaking process that involved watching the interviews with Sam and typing it up as he spoke. I had tried utilising some transcription software to ease the load but because of Sam's hybrid Polish and Mancunian accent, it created more work than it saved, and so I reverted to good, old-fashioned word by word notetaking and typing.

I realised through this process just how distracted I must have been at times when Sam had told me the stories in person, because some of the material I heard in the transcription process I don't remember hearing the first time around.

It took me weeks just to transcribe the first interview we conducted from that very first sitting. Listening so intently, I got to see, hear and feel every little detail of that part of the story. The slow transcription process allowed the story to seep into my mind, and my heart, and the story became more and more a part of my own life.

I would speak with Robbie a couple of times each week and ask about how Sam was doing, and then we would talk about general things - life, family, business, football and everything else. Robbie said that Sam was cheekily asking how I was getting on with the book. I told him about the work I was doing each week to turn the interviews into a written form, and he was delighted to hear that some progress was finally being made to creating the book his dad had always wanted written, and he kept his dad informed.

I felt I needed to manage their expectations to some degree, because the task was enormous, and with my other life commitments I didn't want Sam to expect a finished piece in a matter of weeks. Robbie explained it to Sam, and Sam said he totally understood; he was only winding me up. That was very Sam.

Something was also niggling at me about the shape the transcription was taking. The story was the story as told by Sam, word for word, and I didn't want to mess with that in anyway, but I was also concerned that a straight up transcription of Sam's interviews could potentially dilute the impact of the story, rather than enhance it.

When you watched Sam speak, he was mesmerising. You got to experience all his character and charm, and also feel and see his emotional journey, but even then, twenty hours of interviews was far too long to expect even the most interested viewer to endure.

In written form though, this was even more challenging. Without seeing Sam and being able to watch his visual cues and body language, regardless of how riveting the story was, it could become difficult for the reader to keep reading when it was just someone talking all the time.

This worried me. I had to find a way to break the story up and to help describe for the reader what was happening outside of the actual story Sam was telling. I needed to provide a context, a setting, a time and place - but that would mean putting myself in the story and relating to the reader my experience of Sam telling me his story, something I was uncomfortable to do. I wanted this to be Sam's story and that I was an invisible part of its telling.

I expressed my dilemma with Robbie, and Robbie in turn, discussed this with Sam. Sam totally understood what I was saying, and the answer came back strong and clear from them both, that I had to tell the story of our journey together. They said I was part of the family and part of the story, and it was important to them.

With this confirmation, I set about the simplest telling of my journey with the Gontarz family, around the major event of Sam's incredible story - I was still resolute that I would remain as invisible as possible.

This released me to some degree, from a writer's perspective, and I was able to then write about the wider context and setting of Sam's story. Within a few weeks, I had a draft of the first few chapters and I sent it to Robbie to give to Sam, to see what they thought of it.

A few days later, Robbie returned a copy of the draft to me from Sam.

Although it wouldn't be necessarily right to do so, it would be easy to look at Sam and see this tiny, fragile, ninety-year-old man and think perhaps that he might not be as with it as he was in younger years. That would be totally the wrong way to look at Sam. The copy of the draft that Robbie gave back to me was marked and circled with comments, thoughts, and every single spelling or grammatical error he could find. In my defence, I hadn't checked it too thoroughly just yet. I wanted to know that they approved with my approach first, but I really smiled when I saw just how thorough and focused Sam was.

Besides pointing out these few errors, Sam loved it. He was delighted with the way that the story unfolded, and he loved the way I had set the context for him. I was delighted too, and greatly boosted by his approval.

Robbie mentioned while I was with him that Sam had been asked to attend a few Holocaust events in the next few weeks and months, and that it might be of interest for me to attend with them. I thought it was a great idea. I mentioned to Robbie that maybe I could build a little website for Sam so that he could collect email addresses from people that he met, and that through an email newsletter, he could share some of his stories and keep people informed as to the progress of the book. Robbie loved the idea, but I asked him to run it by Sam before I started doing any work on it.

Robbie called later that night and said his dad was excited by the idea.

Robbie also mentioned that his family were in town at the weekend, and they were all planning to go for dinner locally on Sunday with Sam and Adrian and would we like to join them and finally get everyone together for the first time. Unfortunately, we had plans on Sunday afternoon across town, and it seemed unlikely we would be able to make it, but I said I would stay in touch with Robbie and see how we got on.

Chapter 27

A Significant Meal

I spent the next two whole days putting a website together for Sam. I am far from a web developer but am capable enough to know my way around some of the web developer applications that enable you to drag and drop elements and build a site with some basic knowledge.

I bought the domain <u>www.samgontarz.com</u> and created a simple enough site that briefly teased Sam's story and yet was powerful enough to grab attention and encourage people to sign up for a newsletter, where Sam and the family could send out updates every now and again.

I impressed myself with what I was able to create within the space of a couple of days (and nights), and I sent it on to Sam and Robbie to have a look at.

Several hours later, Robbie called. Sam was blown away by the website. He loved it, was fascinated by it and was deeply grateful to me for creating it.

I was so relieved that he liked it. His approval had come to mean a great deal to me. I was very conscious of being a part of the telling of his story but not wanting to divert it in any way with my ideas, and so when he consented to those ideas, it always meant a lot.

The next day was the Sunday when Robbie and Sam and the family were meeting for a five o'clock early dinner. My family and I were across town visiting my mum, and by late afternoon, it seemed unlikely we were going to make it back in time. We finally arrived home at just gone five o clock, and we were all really tired and just ready to settle down and prepare for school and work the next day. But I had this feeling that we should go and say "hi" to the Gontarz family, as it had already taken over six months for everybody to be in the same town. It seemed a waste of an opportunity.

We got back in the car and drove to the restaurant. We walked in and the restaurant was deserted apart from a big, long table with Sam sat on his own right in the middle. Robbie had seen Sam to his chair and now returned to let his wife Clare and their two kids, Remi and Lucia, out of the car. We introduced everyone to one another and went to join Sam.

Sam motioned for me to sit next to him. I bent down to give him a hug and sat down next to him. My wife, Suzanne, and Clare sat next to each other and began chatting like old friends. My eldest daughter, Tali, sat with Robbie's youngest Lucia - they were the same age and shared a common love of drama, singing and dancing. Needless to say, they got on famously and spent the entire evening in deep discussion, and giggles.

Robbie sat opposite to me and his eldest, Remi, sat opposite his grandpa Sam. Adrian, Robbie's brother, arrived shortly afterwards, and then Robbie's brother and sister-in-law, also over from the Lake District, arrived with their two kids. The restaurant was starting to fill, and just with Sam and his extended friends and family.

The impromptu party was soon completed by the arrival of Hayley, a young student who had just completed her degree dissertation about Holocaust survivors and had become understandably very close to Sam in the process. She sat on Sam's other side, and we all began to discuss various aspects of our projects surrounding Sam's life story.

My youngest, seven-year-old daughter, Danya, was feeling left out, perched on the end of the table and with nobody to play with. Out of nowhere, one of her good friends, Ella, arrived at the restaurant with her mum and dad, and a collection of new toys. Ella's dad, Jason, was the son of a Holocaust survivor too, a man also called Sam. Jason's dad, Sam, had in fact been the one to persuade Sam Gontarz to stay in England when he began to feel unhappy staying at his relatives' house. They became lifelong friends, and Jason was extended family, hence his arrival at the restaurant, and providing the perfect distraction for my youngest with the arrival of Ella. The night was falling into place effortlessly.

The Gontarz family had soon taken over most of the restaurant, and the atmosphere was warm and magical. A few bottles of wine were drunk, the conversation flowed, and the room felt like a true celebration, and Sam was the focus of all that warmth and joy.

At one point, I looked at him and saw that he was beaming from ear to ear. He was just watching everyone in the room and smiling. Everyone he cared most about, and who cared about him, was in that room that night. It was beautiful.

One personal highlight for me during the evening was when Sam turned to me and told me how much he loved the website I had created for him. He pulled me in closer by grabbing my arm and talked louder so I could hear him over the noise in the room,

"Ricky, of everyone I have ever told my story too over all the years, you were the best. I was very comfy with you, and you brought things out of me that I never knew were in there. Thank you."

My heart soared. I felt elated. It was the highest praise and the kindest thing he could have said to me.

He punctuated my elation by saying to me, "Let's Whatsapp tomorrow, so we can discuss the book more."

"You're on Whatsapp?" I asked, surprised.

"Yeah, I love it," he replied, with a smile on his face.

"After a whole year of communicating through Robbie we could have been chatting through Whatsapp? I never knew," I said, tickled by his tech savvy. It hadn't even entered my head but I could have been running ideas directly to Sam. Out of respect, I had just run everything through Robbie.

"I'll message you tomorrow," he said as I lent in to give him a hug, and we said our goodbyes to everyone in the room.

We got in the car, turned it around in the right direction and drove passed the restaurant. We stopped to wave at everyone but they were distracted saying their goodbyes. I noticed Sam sat looking around him at his beloved family, that huge smile upon his face.

I smiled too, and then we drove home.

Chapter 28

Newsletter Sign-Ups

I was at work the next day, sat at my desk doing some writing, and my phone kept pinging with messages. After three or four pings, curiosity got the best of me and I took a look at my phone. There were notifications from the Sam Gontarz website alerting me that people had been signing up for the newsletter. Excited that the site was already gathering traffic, I clicked on the link and it took me to the backend of the website where I was able to see the details of who had signed up for the newsletter, all four of them were Sam Gontarz.

I chuckled to myself. It meant that Sam was visiting his own website, and this gave me an immense sense of pride to know that he was checking it out. I also soon realised that the reason he kept signing up for the newsletter was because the site had a pop-up window that appears after a few seconds of arriving at the site, and the pop-up encourages people to sign up for the newsletter. And, although Sam was incredibly tech savvy for a ninety-year-old, he hadn't quite sussed out that there was a simple 'X' button in the corner of the pop-up which would clear it without having to sign up for the newsletter every time, and so, unknowingly, every time he went to the site he thought he had to sign up.

I thought about calling him to tell him this, but I thought he would probably soon get bored of visiting the site. Over the next few hours, and with my phone pinging seven more times with notifications telling me Sam had signed up again and again, I thought I had better let him know. Again, it made my heart swell with pride to know that Sam was visiting the site over and over again. I felt happy to think that Sam might have realised that this website was something real and tangible and a place where all his stories could be collated and shared with the world, finally.

I messaged him to thank him for last night, and to gently inform him of how to visit the site without signing up for the newsletter each time. I also wanted to clarify some of the comments he had made to the first few chapters of the book that I had sent to him.

He wrote back immediately, "Hi Ricky, good morning to you, yes what a lovely get together last night and meeting your lovely family. I'll have to pick up the pages and read them again to be able to comment on what I had written. I'll be back when I have checked them. Have a good day. xx"

He didn't heed my advice about the website though, I received six more notifications that day that he had signed up for the newsletter.

Chapter 29

Missed Call

A couple of days later, on the Thursday, I was attending an online workshop in my office when I saw a call from Robbie come through. I had ten minutes left on the seminar and so I figured I would let it ring off and call him back then.

When I finished the workshop I dialled his number. He answered immediately. I addressed him in the way we started most of our conversations, "Hi Dude, you okay?"

His voice trembled as he quietly said, "Not really man, dad passed away this morning."

For about a minute, the world went black. I sat with my elbows on my desk, head in my hands and listened to Robbie telling me, through his sobs, about the events that had unfolded at Sam's flat that morning. I couldn't concentrate on what he was saying, but I remember him saying that Adrian had been urgently called by Sheila and had eventually got to Sam, but there wasn't much he could do by that time.

Robbie was crushed. He wept down the phone to me. I took a deep breath and composed myself, then listened quietly while he shared his stories and his memories of his dad, "He was my everything, Ricky. He was my hero. He was my best pal. What am I going to do without him?"

There is just no answer for a question like that.

After I got off the phone to Robbie, I sat in my office and allowed my thoughts and feelings to wash over me. It felt surreal. I was very sad, naturally, and yet I also felt happy that I had got to know this gorgeous little man just ten months earlier. I had been so fortunate to spend a huge part of the year getting to know him deeply and listen to him tell me the tragic story of his life. And then he was gone. Just like that.

***

So, I did what often comes most naturally to me in moments like this, I wrote my thoughts and feelings down in my journal. This is what I wrote at 2.20 pm on Thursday 14th November 2019:

> *I've just got off the phone to Robbie. Sam passed away this morning. I'm in shock. Robbie was crushed. He called he said because he wanted me to know from him directly and because he wanted me to also know that Sunday night had given his dad such a lot of happiness and joy, and that he'd felt like it was one big extended family, the one thing he had sought all his life. Robbie reiterated time and again how much I meant to his dad and how much he had loved sharing his story with me throughout this year.*

> *From a personal point of view, I feel strangely serene and at peace with the timing of everything. I have his entire story down on tape in all its brutal but glorious detail. I was also, serendipitously, moved to create a website for him just last weekend and was*

able to show it to him and see how proud and happy he was with it. It made me laugh because he signed up to the newsletter so many times.

I'm also so privileged that we spoke on Whatsapp only on Monday where we discussed the book and he told me how wonderful it was to meet the family on Sunday. How incredibly graceful that we did make the decision to go to the restaurant on Sunday night.

It's all so graceful really. Robbie and Adrian were able to go back to Poland with Sam in July. We recorded his story this year. He saw the website and loved it. I feel like perhaps he knew his work was done and everything was now taken care of.

Sam, I truly loved spending time with you this year. I am a little embarrassed by my initial reluctance to get involved with you and the telling of your story. Like so many people these days, we get lost and bogged down in the busyness of our lives, and our priorities and perspectives often get skewed in our scheduled daily chaos. I am grateful to the great 'whatever there is/God/The Universe' that I listened to my heart just enough to get in touch with Robbie again and then to make the effort to meet you. Once I did meet you, it wasn't long at all before you opened up my heart with your incredible courage and honesty and that ineffable sparkle that shined so brightly from your eyes.

You showed me that when we open our hearts to even relative strangers, we never know what we can learn, and how they can change our lives forever.

You taught me the magic of truly listening to somebody else's story, without an agenda and without judgement, and what beauty comes from that, when we stop and take the time to just listen.

Getting to know you has been a true pleasure and a dear privilege and thank you for welcoming me into your family. You are an inspiration in every single way. I will never forget the time we spent together. It is something that will stay with me for the rest of my life. The trust you gave to me in opening up your heart with your story was the greatest compliment I could ever hope to receive.

Your story is incredible, and I will do everything that I can to share it with the world, and to keep you and your family alive in our hearts. You have so much to teach the world, and the world needs stories like yours more than ever right now.

I do fear though that even the greatest writer in the world wouldn't be able to do justice to your character, charm, kindness and warmth. The glint in your eye told of both your depth and pain but it was also full of joy, and mischief.

You were cute, kind, warm, funny, open, vulnerable and fiercely brave despite all of the horrors that you had experienced in your life.

Thank you for your honesty and your beautiful heart. I will do all I can to keep your story alive.

I am so happy that we got to meet and spend time together and to call you a friend.

I will miss you.

All my love.

Ricky xx

Chapter 30

Saying Goodbye

The very next day, a huge crowd of friends and family gathered at Southern Cemetery in South Manchester to say their goodbyes to Sam.

It was a beautiful, clear, crisp day - unusual for a Manchester November, but perfectly fitting that the weather would turn out good for Sam.

We gathered in the Ohel, a room where everyone stands before visiting the grave, and Sam's coffin lay on a table in the middle of the room. For such a tiny person, the coffin struck me as huge, and I smiled to think that it was the size of his character that was so much greater than his physical size.

I stood looking at the coffin while we waited for the service to begin, and I thought about all the things that this man had gone through in his life. And, then I thought about how he would now be finally reunited with his family after over seventy-five years, and that thought made me happy and sad at the same time.

Robbie said a few words about his dad, and although he struggled at times to get through it, he spoke beautifully and with incredible courage. Adrian was just very, very sad, and Sheila appeared very frail and weak.

We walked to the graveside in a long, slow procession. Prayers were said and then Sam was gently lowered into the ground, and we all said our goodbyes.

I considered in that moment how he was the only member of his whole family to have ever had a proper, dignified burial.

Epilogue

Never Forget

Just a few weeks after Sam had passed away, there was an event held at Salford University in aid of the Holocaust Memorial Trust, to commemorate seventy-five years since the liberation of Auschwitz. At some point towards the middle of last year, Sam had promised to speak at the event, and in typical Sam style, had already written his speech for the occasion, even though it was months away. But in the light of Sam's passing, rather than cancel the event, Robbie bravely decided that he would attend on behalf of his dad, and even more incredibly, he would read out the speech that his dad had written specifically for that night.

I got to the university early that evening to support Robbie. He was understandably nervous and unsure of whether he would be able to get through the reading, but equally determined to do his dad proud. I encouraged him to just go with whatever he felt, and that everyone in the room was on his side and would understand how difficult it was going to be for him.

The auditorium was packed out. The host for the evening, Councillor Heather Fletcher, explained the running order for the night and asked that out of respect for every speaker, and indeed the subject matter of their talks, could all applause wait until the very end of the evening.

After the brief introduction to the evening, Robbie was called up to the stage. He stood at the lectern and took a deep breath. As he did this, two giant screens suddenly lit up above his head displaying a huge picture of Sam. The room gasped.

It was a good job Robbie couldn't see it.

I had seen the picture before, it was the picture of Sam from his recent trip to Poland with Robbie and Adrian. It was the one where he was sat eating dinner in the square, where as a child he had been banned for being a Jew. Sam himself had described this moment of freedom and being able to return to this site with his sons as one of the happiest moments of his life. He had a huge smile on his face in this picture and I couldn't help but smile looking at him, as his face, quite literally, lit up the room from the screens above.

Robbie breathed deeply and began to speak: "My name is Robbie Gontarz, and I am the proud son of Holocaust survivor, Sam Gontarz. My father was due to speak to you tonight, as he had a passion for using his experience to educate the world, so that what he, and millions like him suffered, never happens again. Unfortunately, my wonderful father passed away a few weeks ago, but I would like to read his words to you now, so that his voice lives on."

Robbie somehow had got through his opening paragraph, but he broke down at this point, and stood at the lectern and cried. There was a strange feeling in the room though; it was as if everybody in there was sending him love and encouragement through their sheer willpower. You could feel it, total electricity in the room. He gathered himself together, wiped his eyes and began to tell Sam's story.

At times, the room was pin-drop silent, almost like everybody was holding their breath collectively. Robbie read his dad's words slowly and clearly, injecting the story with passion and anger at the moments when he himself felt the injustice of the things that had happened to his dad, and members of their family.

At the part when Sam was reunited with his sister Sala, in the displaced persons camp after they were liberated, the room burst into applause. At the moment when she was killed in the road accident several months later, the room collectively gasped and deflated.

Sam's speech built to a powerful crescendo, and Robbie's intensity added to the power of this. At the end of the speech, although requested not to at the start of the evening, the room erupted into a prolonged, spontaneous standing ovation and rapturous applause. Robbie was taken aback by the response. He looked around him bewildered, wondering what he had done to deserve such appreciation. Both his strength, and his vulnerability, had captured everybody's hearts in a deep, powerful and beautiful way. Sam would have been very, very proud.

Robbie worked his way back to his seat, shaking hands with people who had risen from their seats and moved down the aisles hoping to pass on their support and appreciation for the incredibly brave job he had just done. Eventually, when he got back to his seat and sat down, he looked back up at the stage and for the first time, he saw the picture of his dad beaming down from the screens above, and at that point he broke down. I was sat a few rows back and to the right-hand side of the auditorium but I could see he had his head in his hands and his shoulders were shaking as he sobbed away the sadness, and the relief washed over him.

Heather Fletcher took to the stage and thanked Robbie sincerely, commending his bravery and strength, and complimenting the powerful words of his dad. She then introduced the BBC Philharmonic String Quartet who had been quietly taking their places on the stage behind her. I'm not sure if it was an accident or on purpose but as the quartet began to play the opening bars of Elgar's *Serenade For Strings*, the picture of Sam remained on the screens above, and with that there was, literally, not a dry eye in the house. I sat with goosebumps and chills for the entire piece, and tears rolling down my face, looking up at Sam smiling so proudly from above as this heavenly music filled the auditorium.

Afterwards, as Robbie and I walked to the car, I asked him if I could have a copy of the speech, and immediately, Robbie handed me the copy he had in his pocket. I had been puzzling over an ending to the book, and struggling for quite a while to be quite honest, but as Robbie read the final paragraphs of Sam's speech that evening, I knew that I had my ending, and, most appropriately, it would be Sam who would have the last word:

I was one of approximately two hundred and seventy survivors, from thousands leaving Auschwitz on the death marches.

My father died in Lodz ghetto in 1942. My mother was murdered by the Nazis in Auschwitz. My brother was shot whilst trying to escape on a death march. My sister Sala survived in Bergen-Belsen but died in a road accident months later.

May they rest in peace.

I am now ninety-years-old but the memory is as strong in my mind as the tattoo on my arm, B7965.

I saw first-hand what so called intelligent people could do to their fellow man. I saw the very worst of mankind.

How could all this have happened?

How?

I ask myself this time and time again.

If the world was silent then, we must never allow silence now. Remember my words as a survivor of the Holocaust, as testimony of the darkest time in human history.

Let us all be more tolerant, understanding, and never stay silent again: and may we live in a better world than we did.

Let us create a society free of hatred where respect for each other glows, like a beautiful ember.

We must never forget.

Acknowledgements

To my three beautiful girls - Su, Tali, and Danya. I couldn't have done this without your love and your support. I love you more than words could ever express. Thank you for being you and for being there.

Robbie, Clare, Remi, Lucia, and Adrian and the Gontarz family - thank you for trusting me with your dad's precious story. That trust meant more than anything to me, and I only hope that I have repaid that trust with an authentic and realistic portrayal of his incredible story.

Thank you to all those beautiful family and friends who have been on this incredible journey with me through life, and who have played such a significant part in helping me to become the person that I am today. Thank you from the bottom of my heart. You know who you are, and though this dedication may not name you individually, please know that your name is etched in my heart with the deepest love and gratitude for the part you have played in my life, and I am so grateful to share this lifetime with you.

And special thank you to Lionel Ross, the publisher and proprietor of i2i publishing, and to his senior editor, Mark Cripps, for their hard work and support in making this book real, and for bringing my vision to life.

About the Author

Rik Arron is a writer, a poet, and a storyteller. He is a husband and father of two daughters. He runs a family business with his brother, and is the co-founder of a radio station, *The Buzz Mcr.*

Rik is the author of two illustrated children's poetry books, *Chasing Rainbows* and *Billy Stink's Incredible Circus.*

He spends much of his spare time helping people to tell their stories and write their books via in-person or online workshops.

Also, Rik is a passionate advocate of meditation, personal growth, and the spiritual path.

Contact details
Email address: rik@rikarron.co.uk
Website: www.rikarron.co.uk
Instagram: rikarron